SCHOLASTIC
LITERACY SKILLS

Spelling
Year 6

TERMS AND CONDITIONS

IMPORTANT – PERMITTED USE AND WARNINGS – READ CAREFULLY BEFORE USING

Copyright in the software contained in this CD-ROM and in its accompanying material belongs to Scholastic Limited. All rights reserved. © 2009 Scholastic Ltd.

Save for these purposes, or as expressly authorised in the accompanying materials, the software may not be copied, reproduced, used, sold, licensed, transferred, exchanged, hired, or exported in whole or in part or in any manner or form without the prior written consent of Scholastic Ltd. Any such unauthorised use or activities are prohibited and may give rise to civil liabilities and criminal prosecutions.

The material contained on this CD-ROM may only be used in the context for which it was intended in *Scholastic Literacy Skills*, and is for use only in the school which has purchased the book and CD-ROM, or by the teacher who has purchased the book and CD-ROM. Permission to download images is given for purchasers only and not for users from any lending service. Any further use of the material contravenes Scholastic Ltd's copyright and that of other rights holders.

This CD-ROM has been tested for viruses at all stages of its production. However, we recommend that you run virus-checking software on your computer systems at all times. Scholastic Ltd cannot accept any responsibility for any loss, disruption or damage to your data or your computer system that may occur as a result of using either the CD-ROM or the data held on it.

IF YOU ACCEPT THE ABOVE CONDITIONS YOU MAY PROCEED TO USE THE CD-ROM.

Minimum system requirements:

- PC or Mac with CD-ROM drive (16x speed recommended) and 512MB RAM
- P4 or G4 processor
- Windows 2000/XP/Vista or Mac OSX 10.3 to 10.6

For all technical support queries, please phone Scholastic Customer Services on 0845 6039091.

Author
Gillian Howell

Development Editor
Rachel Mackinnon

Editor
Sally Gray

Assistant editors
Jennie Clifford and Alex Albrighton

CD-ROM design and development team
Joy Monkhouse, Anna Oliwa,
Micky Pledge, Rebecca Male, Allison Parry,
James Courier, Jim Peacock/Beehive Illustration
and Haremi

Series designers
Shelley Best and Anna Oliwa

Book designers
Shelley Best and Andrea Lewis

Illustrations
Rupert Van Wyk/Beehive Illustration

Designed using Adobe Indesign
Published by Scholastic Ltd, Book End,
Range Road, Witney,
Oxfordshire OX29 0YD
www.scholastic.co.uk

Printed by Bell & Bain Ltd, Glasgow
Text © 2009 Gillian Howell
© 2009 Scholastic Ltd
2 3 4 5 6 7 8 9 0   2 3 4 5 6 7 8

British Library Cataloguing-in-Publication Data
A catalogue record for this book is available from
the British Library.
ISBN 978-1407-10059-3

The right of Gillian Howell to be identified as the author
of this work has been asserted by her in accordance with
the Copyright, Designs and Patents Act 1988.

All rights reserved. This book is sold subject to the
condition that it shall not, by way of trade or otherwise,
be lent, hired out or otherwise circulated without the
publisher's prior consent in any form of binding or cover
other than that in which it is published and without
a similar condition, including this condition, being
imposed upon the subsequent purchaser.

No part of this publication may be reproduced, stored
in a retrieval system, or transmitted, in any form or
by any means, electronic, mechanical, photocopying,
recording or otherwise, other than for the purposes
described in the lessons in this book, without
the prior permission of the publisher. This book
remains copyright, although permission is granted
to copy pages where indicated for classroom
distribution and use only in the school which has
purchased the book, or by the teacher who has
purchased the book, and in accordance with
the CLA licensing agreement. Photocopying
permission is given only for purchasers and
not for borrowers of books from any lending
service.

Every effort has been made to trace copyright holders for the
works reproduced in this book, and the publishers apologize for
any inadvertent omissions.

Extracts from Primary National Strategy's Primary Framework for
Literacy (2006) www.standards.dfes.gov.uk/primaryframework ©
Crown copyright. Reproduced under the terms of the Click Use
Licence.

Contents

Introduction

The Scholastic Literacy Skills: Spelling series

Learning to spell depends on much more than simply memorising words. Exercises, word lists and tests are not enough. Children need to actively engage in the process, tackling new words using knowledge and skills acquired, taking risks and making errors. Purposeful writing is a key to learning to spell. Children need to see spelling as a useful tool for communication (rather than a rod to be beaten with!). To study the spelling of words we need to take them out of context but context is needed to learn how to use them and to give purpose for using them.

This series provides a bank of adaptable ideas and resources for teaching spelling. Each chapter is, to some extent, independent of the others and chapters do not, therefore, always need to be followed in order. Activities within a section sometimes build upon each other and should be followed sequentially. It is anticipated that sections and activities will be selected as required to fit in with medium term planning for each term.

Overview of the teaching of spelling

In English the relationship between sounds and letters (phonics) has been complicated by the complex history of the English language and there is not a simple one-to-one correspondence. Despite this complexity, a great deal of the relationship between letters and sounds is rule-bound, which means phonics works, but not all of the time. There is logic and pattern but there are also 'oddities'.

However spelling does not only represent sound; it also represents grammar and meaning. For example, the '-ed' suffix that identifies regular past-tense verbs can be pronounced /d/ or /id/ or /t/ but never /ed/, but it is always spelled 'ed'. If spelling only represented sound, different accents would require different spellings. Instead of viewing the complexity as a problem, perhaps we might more usefully celebrate the richness and resourcefulness of English spelling.

Teaching spelling involves drawing children's attention to patterns: patterns of sounds and letters, patterns related to grammatical functions and patterns related to word origin. Although English spelling does have 'rules', such as 'q' is always followed by 'u', it is much more realistic to talk about patterns, conventions, possibilities and probabilities. Many so-called rules have so many exceptions or are so complex to explain, that they are not worth teaching. To teach something as a rule which is later contradicted is not helpful. Children become active, constructive learners by investigating and generalising common patterns, and acknowledging exceptions.

About the product

This book contains seven chapters of activities for teaching spelling. Each chapter focuses on a different aspect of spelling knowledge or skills, and is organised into three sections with clear objectives, background information for the concepts taught, teaching ideas, and photocopiable pages for use in whole class teaching, with groups or for independent work. Each chapter also features a poster and assessment section. The General activities section at the end of the book provides a set of generic games, activities and circle times linked to the activities in this book.

Posters

Each chapter has one poster. These posters are related to the subject of the chapter and should be displayed and used for reference throughout the work on the chapter. The poster notes (on the chapter opening page) offer suggestions for how they could be used. There are black and white versions in the book and full-colour versions on the CD-ROM for you to print out or display on your whiteboard.

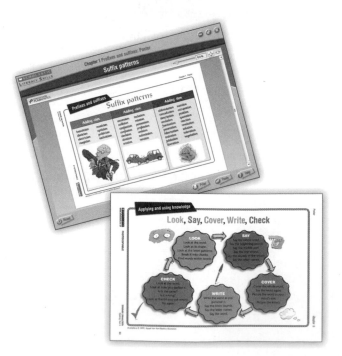

Assessment

Each chapter concludes with an assessment section. It summarises the objectives and activities in the section, provides pointers on observation and record keeping and includes one assessment photocopiable page (which is also printable from the CD-ROM with answers, where appropriate).

Activities

Each section contains three to four activities. These activities all take the form of a photocopiable page which is in the book. Each photocopiable page is also included on the CD-ROM for you to display or print out (these pages are also provides with answers where appropriate). Over thirty of the photocopiable pages have linked interactive activities on the CD-ROM. These interactive activities are designed to act as starter activities to the lesson, giving whole-class support on the information being taught. However, they can also work equally well as plenary activities, reviewing the work the children have just completed.

Differentiation

Activities in this book are not differentiated explicitly, although teacher notes may make suggestions for support or extension. Many of the activities can be used with the whole class with extra support provided through differentiated and open-ended questions, use of additional adults, mixed-ability paired or group work or additional input and consolidation before and/or after lessons. Some children may need support with the reading aspects of tasks in order to participate in the spelling objectives.

Using the CD-ROM

Below are brief guidance notes for using the CD-ROM. For more detailed information, see **How to use** on the start-up screen, or **Help** on the relevant screen for information about that page.

The CD-ROM follows the structure of the book and contains:

- All of the photocopiable pages.
- All of the poster pages in full colour.
- Photocopiable pages (with answers where appropriate).
- Over thirty interactive on-screen activities linked to the photocopiable pages.

Getting started

To begin using the CD-ROM, simply place it in your CD- or DVD-ROM drive. Although the CD-ROM should auto-run, if it fails to do so, navigate to the drive and double-click on the red **Start** icon.

Start-up screen

The start-up screen is the first screen that appears. Here you can access: terms and conditions, registration links, how to use the CD-ROM and credits. If you agree to the terms and conditions, click **Start** to continue.

Main menu

The main menu provides links to all of the chapters or all of the resources. Clicking on the relevant **Chapter** icon will take you to the chapter screen where you can access the posters and the chapter's sections. Clicking on **All resources** will take you to a list of all the resources, where you can search by key word or chapter for a specific resource.

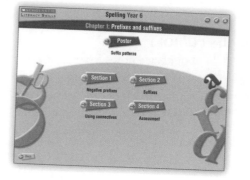

Section screen

Upon choosing a section from the chapter screen, you are taken to a list of resources for that section. Here you can access all of the photocopiable pages related to that section as well as the linked interactive activities.

Resource finder

The **Resource finder** lists all of the resources on the CD-ROM. You can:

- Select a chapter and/or section by selecting the appropriate title from the drop-down menus.
- Search for key words by typing them into the search box.
- Scroll up or down the list of resources to locate the required resource.
- To launch a resource, simply click on its row on the screen.

Navigation

The resources (poster pages, photocopiable pages and interactive activities) all open in separate windows on top of the menu screen. This means that you can have more than one resource open at the same time. To close a resource, click on the **x** in the top right-hand corner of the screen. To return to the menu screen you can either close or minimise a resource.

Closing a resource will not close the program. However, if you are in a menu screen, then clicking on the **x** will close the program. To return to a previous menu screen, you need to click on the **Back** button.

Whiteboard tools

The CD-ROM comes with its own set of whiteboard tools for use on any whiteboard. These include:

- Pen tool
- Highlighter tool
- Eraser
- Sticky note

Click on the **Tools** button at the foot of the screen to access these tools.

Printing

Print the resources by clicking on the **Print** button. The photocopiable pages print as full A4 portrait pages, but please note if you have a landscape photocopiable page or poster you need to set the orientation to landscape in your print preferences. The interactive activities will print what is on the screen. For a full A4 printout you need to set the orientation to landscape in your print preferences.

Top tips

Use these top tips to help your children learn to spell effectively.

Look for patterns and exceptions when reading and writing.

Use personal spelling journals, proofreading (with a partner), and dictionaries.

Use ICT to investigate spellings.

Use plastic letters and computers to explore spelling patterns without the physical demands of letter formation.

Use teacher-led investigations which encourage children to 'see' the rule or convention for themselves.

Look, Say, Cover, Write, Check.

Carry out regular spelling tests.

Use individual whiteboards regularly – this enables children to correct mistakes and to use peer support.

In writing encourage children to 'have a go' at spellings to maintain the train of thought and then check later.

Combine cursive handwriting lessons with spelling to reinforce common letter strings.

When marking, celebrate what is right and then look for patterns of errors to target teaching.

Use word banks with caution – you do not learn how to spell a word by copying.

Make spelling activities multi-sensory to capitalise on different learning styles.

Make spelling fun: play sound, rhyme and letter games, and do word puzzles, crosswords and wordsearches.

When marking spelling in different curriculum areas, focus on the current spelling rule or convention being taught.

Framework objectives

Chapter	Page	Section	Literacy skills objective	Strand 6: Spell familiar words correctly and employ a range of strategies to spell difficult and unfamiliar words.	Strand 6: Use a range of appropriate strategies to edit, proofread and correct spelling in their own work, on paper and on screen.	Strand 6: (progression into Year 7) Revise, consolidate and secure knowledge of correct vowel choices, pluralisation, prefixes, word endings and high frequency words.	Strand 6: (progression into Year 7) Draw on analogies to known words, roots, derivations, word families, morphology and familiar spelling patterns.
Chapter 1	12	Negative prefixes	To investigate the addition of prefixes to root words as an aid to spelling using 'dis-', 'in-', 'im-', 'il-', 'ir-', 'un-' and 'mis-'.	✓		✓	
	16	Suffixes	To use root words and suffixes '-ible', '-able', '-cian', '-sion', '-tion' as an aid to spelling.	✓		✓	
	20	Using connectives	To investigate the spellings of connectives.	✓			
Chapter 2	28	Word families	To identify word roots, derivations and spelling patterns.	✓			✓
	32	Greek and Latin words	To use word roots with prefixes and suffixes that originate from Greek and Latin words.	✓			✓
	36	Borrowed words	To investigate the use of words that originated in other parts of the world.	✓			✓
Chapter 3	44	Inflections and rules	To spell words with inflectional endings '-ed' and '-ing', '-er' and '-est' for words ending in 'e' or 'y'. To invent own rules for pluralising nouns.	✓	✓		
	48	Terminology	To become familiar with the meaning and use of terms used to talk about spelling and language.	✓		✓	✓
	52	Transforming words	To extend work using suffixes and prefixes by changing nouns to verbs and verbs to nouns.	✓		✓	
Chapter 4	60	Rule or exception?	To investigate and learn a range of spelling rules and their exceptions.	✓		✓	✓
	65	Unstressed vowels	To investigate and learn the spellings of words with unstressed vowels.	✓		✓	✓
	70	Establishing rules	To learn and invent a range of spelling rules.	✓			✓

Framework objectives

Chapter	Page	Section	Literacy skills objective	Strand 6: Spell familiar words correctly and employ a range of strategies to spell difficult and unfamiliar words.	Strand 6: Use a range of appropriate strategies to edit, proofread and correct spelling in their own work, on paper and on screen.	Strand 6: (progression into Year 7) Revise, consolidate and secure knowledge of correct vowel choices, pluralisation, prefixes, word endings and high frequency words.	Strand 6: (progression into Year 7) Draw on analogies to known words, roots, derivations, word families, morphology and familiar spelling patterns.
Chapter 5	78	Phonemes and syllables	To use phonemes and syllables to learn the spelling of longer tricky words.	✓			
Chapter 5	82	Long vowel sounds	To revise the spelling of long vowel phonemes.	✓		✓	
Chapter 5	86	Words within words	To use words within words as an aid to spelling longer words.	✓			✓
Chapter 6	94	Letter strings	To revise the spelling of words with letter strings '-ant', '-ance', '-ent', '-ence', 'our' and '-ure'.	✓		✓	
Chapter 6	98	Tricky spellings	To secure the spelling of words with silent letters, 'ie' and 'ei' spelling patterns and contracted verbs.	✓		✓	
Chapter 6	102	Making analogies	To practise spelling using analogies with known words. To use visual and aural strategies to aid spelling.	✓			✓
Chapter 7	110	Confusables	To secure the spelling and meaning of easily confused words.	✓		✓	
Chapter 7	114	Editing, prefixes and suffixes	To practise editing a passage of writing. To revise the conventions for adding prefixes 'un-', 'im-', 'mis-', 'dis-', and suffixes '-ness', '-ity' and '-y' to root words.	✓	✓	✓	
Chapter 7	118	Memory-joggers	To use mnemonics as an aid to remember how to spell words.	✓			✓

Chapter 1
Prefixes and suffixes

Introduction

This chapter focuses on the spellings of words that have prefixes and suffixes, and the spelling and use of connectives. It explores how the addition of prefixes can alter the meaning of the root word by negation. Children's understanding of the meanings of the roots, prefixes and suffixes is emphasised throughout the chapter. The chapter finishes with an activity focusing on connectives and their different uses with an emphasis on how the choice of which connective to use is affected by its purpose.

In this chapter

Negative prefixes page 12	To investigate the addition of prefixes to root words as an aid to spelling, using 'dis-', 'in-', 'im-', 'il-', 'ir-', 'un-' and 'mis-'.
Suffixes page 16	To use root words and suffixes '-ible', '-able', '-cian', '-sion', '-tion' as an aid to spelling.
Using connectives page 20	To investigate the spellings of connectives.
Assessment page 24	Activities and ideas to assess knowledge of prefixes and suffixes.

Poster notes

Suffix patterns (page 11)

Display this poster as an aid to the children when they are exploring the spelling of words with suffixes.

Read the words in each column together and discuss the word class (nouns) and their root words. Encourage the children to find any patterns they can as this will help them to work out and remember their own rules. (For example, the root of *evolution* is 'evolve'; the root of *solution* is 'solve'; thus the pattern where verbs ending in '-lve' drop the final 'e' and add 'u' before the '-tion' suffix can be discovered.) Encourage the children to use sticky notes to add further words they encounter in their reading to the columns. This will build up their vocabulary while reinforcing their knowledge of the root words and how the suffixes affect the root words when they are added.

Prefixes and suffixes

Suffix patterns

Adding -cian	Adding -sion	Adding -tion	
beautician	ascension	inclusion	abbreviation	mention
dietician	collision	mission	cancellation	occupation
electrician	confession	possession	description	position
magician	confusion	profession	evolution	quotation
musician	decision	revision	fascination	reaction
optician	division	submission	generation	revolution
politician	erosion	tension	hibernation	solution
technician			imitation	toleration
			jubilation	vegetation
			liberation	

Illustrations © 2009, Rupert Van Wyk/Beehive Illustration.

Negative prefixes

Objective

To investigate the addition of prefixes to root words as an aid to spelling, using 'dis-', 'in-', 'im-', 'il-', 'ir-', 'un-' and 'mis-'.

Background knowledge

In these activities children will explore the use of some negative prefixes and will discover that there are some useful rules and patterns that will help their spelling. The prefixes listed in the grid below can be added to the beginning of a root word to change its meaning into the opposite. Point out that there is no adjustment made for double letters (such as *'un-' plus 'natural' = unnatural; 'im-' plus 'mature' = immature*).

Prefix	Use	Example
'un-' and 'in-'	the most common negative prefixes	*un + likely = unlikely* *in + exact = inexact*
'im-'	often used with words beginning with 'm' or 'p'*	*im + mature = immature* *im + patient = impatient*
'il-'	only used for words beginning with 'l'*	*il + legal = illegal*
'ir-'	only used for words beginning with 'r'	*ir + regular = irregular*
'mis-'	alters the meaning of the root to show a mistake is made	*mis + placed = misplaced*
'dis-'	alters the meaning to show a change or difference	*dis + placed = displaced*

*Although 'il-' and 'im-' can only be used with the letters shown, other prefixes can also be used with these letters such as 'un-'.

Activities

Although the rules for adding negative prefixes can be useful, the most effective way to learn is through exposure and usage of prefix antonyms.

● **Photocopiable page 13 'Which negative prefix?'**
In this activity the children are given a list of words with the choice of seven different prefixes that change their meanings from positive to negative. Encourage the children to try out different ideas, checking whether the word they have made looks and sounds right. As a plenary, challenge them to make up their own rule for remembering when to use ' il-' and 'ir-'.

● **Photocopiable page 14 'Opposite sentences'**
In this activity the children will have to identify which words can have negative prefixes added to them, and will then use the new words in context to create sentences with opposite meanings, thus reinforcing the meaning and the spelling pattern. At the end of the activity, write up the words for the children to check their spellings: *irregular, inaudible, unable, inexperienced, immobile, discontented*.

● **Photocopiable page 15 'Prefix search'**
Check that the children are familiar with wordsearches and tell them to watch out for the 'red herrings'. Identify and discuss the red herrings, confirm the spellings of the 12 words and then challenge the children to learn them using the Look, Say, Cover, Write, Check strategy.

Further ideas

● **Root and prefix:** Create cards of the root words and the prefixes from the photocopiable sheets. Ask the children to match the cards to create words.
● **Expanding vocabulary:** From reading, collect other examples of words with negative prefixes, such as 'non-', 'anti-', 'mal-' and 'de-'.

What's on the CD-ROM

On the CD-ROM you will find:
● Printable versions of all three photocopiable pages.
● Answers to all three photocopiable pages.
● Interactive version of 'Which negative prefix?'.

Negative prefixes

Which negative prefix?

■ Adding a prefix can change the meaning of a word from positive to negative, such as: happy/unhappy; contented/discontented.

■ Choose a prefix to add to these words to change them from positive words to negative words.

| un | dis | im | il | in | ir | mis |

Original word	+ prefix	Original word	+ prefix
appearance		rational	
patient		legal	
perfect		accurate	
responsible		visible	
mature		decision	
behave		associate	
possess		passive	
literate		natural	
regular		calculate	
decided		lead	
logical		likely	

Illustrations © 2009, Rupert Van Wyk/Beehive Illustration.

SCHOLASTIC
www.scholastic.co.uk   **PHOTOCOPIABLE**   **Scholastic Literacy Skills**
                                                                     Spelling: Year 6   **13**

Name:

Negative prefixes

Opposite sentences

■ Write a new sentence to give each of these sentences the opposite meaning by adding a prefix to one of the words.

■ Write a new sentence of your own that uses the same word with the prefix.

The bus to school always comes at regular times.

1 _____

2 _____

The actor in the play spoke in an audible voice.

1 _____

2 _____

If Tariq does not finish his homework he will be able to go out later.

1 _____

2 _____

The driver was very experienced and crashed the car.

1 _____

2 _____

Since the wheels fell off, my skateboard has been mobile.

1 _____

2 _____

Everyone felt contented with the outcome of the experiment.

1 _____

2 _____

Illustrations © 2009, Rupert Van Wyk/Beehive Illustration.

PHOTOCOPIABLE

■SCHOLASTIC
www.scholastic.co.uk

Negative prefixes

Prefix search

■ Hidden in the wordsearch are 12 words that all begin with the prefixes **dis-**, **un-**, **il-**, **ir-**, or **im-**. Use different colours to highlight each word then write them as a list at the bottom of the page.

l	n	d	i	s	a	d	v	a	n	t	a	g	e	k
o	m	i	s	s	q	i	r	v	a	o	m	p	w	l
a	d	s	n	r	u	s	k	o	l	i	l	i	p	r
n	r	b	u	u	n	p	o	p	u	l	a	r	o	t
u	n	e	a	g	x	l	b	a	n	l	m	r	r	u
b	i	l	l	i	t	e	r	a	t	e	t	e	h	c
l	p	i	n	r	e	a	s	p	i	g	u	f	s	b
i	l	e	o	d	i	s	z	e	m	a	g	u	s	q
h	i	f	y	e	m	u	n	d	i	l	u	t	e	d
j	m	i	s	c	p	r	e	i	m	a	d	a	z	c
u	i	m	p	u	r	e	t	e	p	k	o	b	b	b
q	v	p	a	s	h	l	i	m	r	d	s	l	y	i
u	t	e	d	i	s	c	o	l	o	u	r	e	d	p
v	s	i	l	o	e	o	d	u	p	n	i	y	a	u
h	s	w	o	n	u	n	s	t	e	a	d	y	o	l
k	f	u	l	h	p	h	q	i	r	i	r	l	u	o

Notes

Suffixes

Objective

To use root words and suffixes '-ible', '-able', '-cian', '-sion', '-tion' as an aid to spelling.

Background knowledge

Adding a suffix to a word modifies its meaning and changes its word class. It often alters the spelling of the root word.

Explain that the suffixes '-ible' and '-able' can be added to verbs to change them into adjectives (for example, *teach/teachable* and *move/movable*). There is no fixed rule to tell you when to use '-able' or '-ible'. Help the children to work out which spelling to use by asking them if they can split the word into a phrase that describes its meaning beginning with 'able' (for example, *usable = able to be used*). Most words ending '-ible' cannot be split in this way (such as *possible*). (See 'Common feature' table.)

Explain to the children that '-ion' is the most common spelling of words that end in a 'shun' sound. The choice of '-sion' or '-tion' depends on the spelling of the root word. Most words ending in '-cian' are words used to name a job or profession (see 'Suffix' table).

Common feature	Example
Most words ending with 'e' drop the 'e' when adding '-able'	*move → movable*
Most words with a soft 'g' or 's' sound use '-ible'	*illegible, possible*
Most words with a hard 'c' or 'g' sound use '-able'	*navigable, despicable*

Suffix	Common rule	Example
'-cian'	names a job	*politician*
'-tion'	● changes a verb into a noun ● sometimes alters root word spelling ● is the most used suffix	*act* (verb) → *action* (noun) *describe →* *description*
'-sion'	● changes a verb into a noun ● used with root words ending 'd', 'de', 's' or 'se'	*confuse* (verb) → *confusion* (noun) *explode →* *explosion*

Activities

● **Photocopiable page 17 'i or a?'**
Discuss the general rules for adding '-ible' or '-able' with the children before they begin. Discuss any patterns that they noticed when they change verbs into adjectives.

● **Photocopiable page 18 'Spot the imposters'**
Probability is an important part of learning to spell and children are given the opportunity to develop this systematically by grouping words according to their patterns.

● **Photocopiable page 19 'Which shun?'**
Children group words according to their spelling pattern. Patterns are reinforced and the children are encouraged to make up a rule to help them remember.

Further ideas

● **Rules and exceptions:** Encourage the children to describe a rule for adding one of the suffixes. Create a weekly word wall with the rule written on it. Children then add words during the week that fit the rule.

What's on the CD-ROM

On the CD-ROM you will find:
● Printable versions of all three photocopiable pages.
● Answers to all three photocopiable pages.
● Interactive versions of all three photocopiable pages.

Name:

Suffixes

i or a?

■ Write **i** or **a** in the space in each of these words.

flex_____ble   us_____ble   desir_____ble

port_____ble   drink_____ble   ed_____ble

horr_____ble   ignor_____ble   suit_____ble

cred_____ble   reli_____ble   profit_____ble

vis_____ble   depend_____ble   avoid_____ble

lik_____ble   sens_____ble   aud_____ble

touch_____ble   consider_____ble

■ Now check them with a dictionary. Rewrite any that were incorrect and learn them using Look, Say, Cover, Write, Check. Can you think of one rule to help you remember how to spell them?

_____

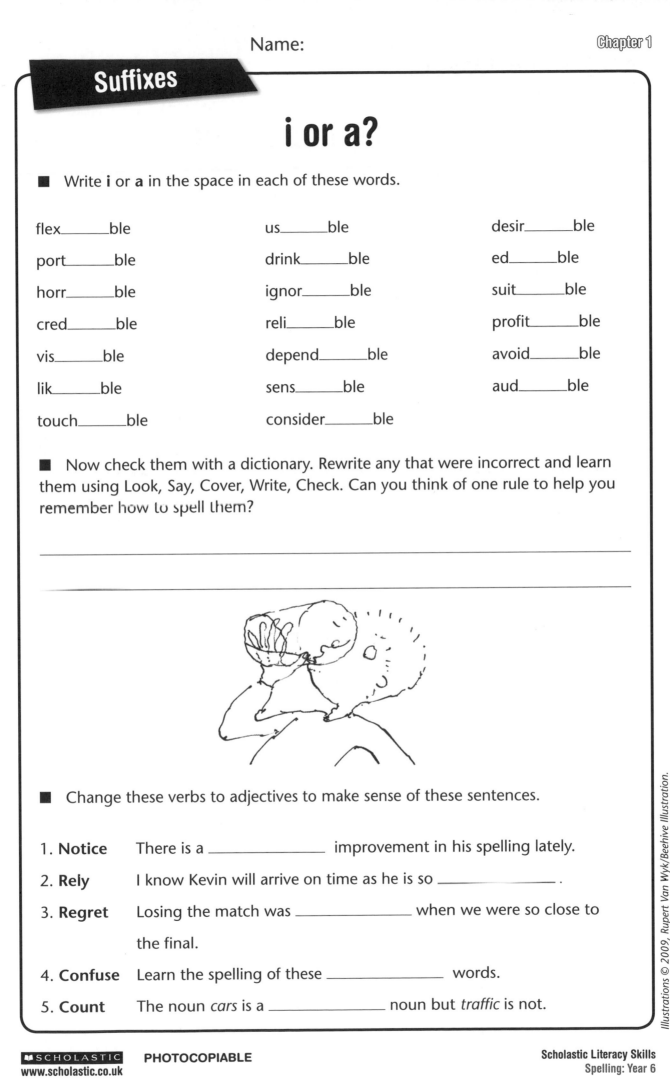

■ Change these verbs to adjectives to make sense of these sentences.

1. **Notice**   There is a _____ improvement in his spelling lately.

2. **Rely**   I know Kevin will arrive on time as he is so _____ .

3. **Regret**   Losing the match was _____ when we were so close to the final.

4. **Confuse**   Learn the spelling of these _____ words.

5. **Count**   The noun *cars* is a _____ noun but *traffic* is not.

SCHOLASTIC
www.scholastic.co.uk   **PHOTOCOPIABLE**

Illustrations © 2009, Rupert Van Wyk/Beehive Illustration.

Name:

Suffixes

Spot the imposters

■ Put the correct words into each column.

■ Beware! Four words are spelled incorrectly. Cross them out!

impossible	probable	usable
illegible	acceptable	laughable
edible	comparable	adjustible
adjustable	valuable	desirable
acceptible	incredible	changeable
drinkable	desirible	movable
changable	eligible	

Words that end with -**ible**	Words that end with -**able**

PHOTOCOPIABLE

■SCHOLASTIC
www.scholastic.co.uk

Suffixes

Which shun?

■ These words are mixed together. Sort them into the correct shape. Can you think of any rules to help you remember which suffix to use?

-cian

-sion

-tion

possession   electrician   revolution   division

politician   confusion

collision   description   magician

mission   caution

reaction

foundation   action   position   direction

extension   musician   optician   relation

decision

■ Sometimes the root word has to be changed. Write the root words for these words.

revolution _____   description _____

decision _____   collision _____

division _____   extension _____

Using connectives

Objective

To investigate the spellings of connectives.

Background knowledge

Connectives are words or phrases that are used to link clauses and sentences; they can be conjunctions, adverbs, or adverbial phrases and they have a variety of uses (see grid below).

Use	Connectives
introducing a similar idea	also, besides, furthermore, in addition, moreover
comparing things or ideas	also, likewise, similarly, and, both… and, not only… but also, neither… nor
opposing or contrasting ideas	alternatively, however, in contrast, instead, in comparison, meanwhile, nevertheless, nonetheless, while, notwithstanding, on the other hand, on the contrary, but, yet, although, even though, though, whereas
showing a cause, effect or result	accordingly, after, as a result, as a consequence, because, consequently, hence, henceforward, if… then, later, thus, therefore, so, since, whenever
showing a sequence or passage of time	after, afterwards, eventually, first, firstly, finally, later, next, then
concluding	finally, in conclusion, to summarise

Activities

● **Photocopiable page 21 'Connecting sentences'**
Find out what the children understand by the term *connectives*. Ask them for some examples, in isolation and then as part of a sentence. Spell them together. When completing the photocopiable sheet the children will be given the opportunity to write the connectives while considering their meanings as an aid to spelling.

● **Photocopiable page 22 'Making connectives'**
Many connectives are compound words. Explain that the spelling rules that apply to compound words also apply to compound connectives (for example, *nevertheless* = never+the+less). The spelling of each component word in the compound word remains the same. In this activity the children generate compound words by combining words from a word bank and writing them in a list to learn using the Look, Say, Cover, Write, Check strategy.

● **Photocopiable page 23 'Tricky connectives'**
Some of the connectives with more tricky spellings are listed for children to practise spelling using Look, Say, Cover, Write, Check on a separate piece of paper. There is also a paragraph with spellings for the children to correct. This encourages them to use visual strategies to check spellings ('Does it look right?').

Further ideas

● **Connective collection:** Create a wall chart with six columns: Introducing, Comparing, Contrasting, Cause and effect, Time, Conclusion. The children collect connectives from reading and add them to the appropriate column.

● **Connective cards:** Create sets of word cards that can be used to make compound connectives. The children can play a version of Pelmanism with a set of the cards. When they turn over two cards that can make a connective, these are removed.

What's on the CD-ROM

On the CD-ROM you will find:
● Printable versions of all three photocopiable pages.
● Answers to all three photocopiable pages.
● Interactive versions of all three photocopiable pages.

Using connectives

Connecting sentences

■ If you can spell and use a range of different connectives, your writing will be much more interesting! Choose a connective from the word bank to fill in the gaps in these sentences.

although	but	whereas
meanwhile	later	despite
that	first	whenever
alternatively	finally	furthermore

1. He rushed through the work _____ he really should have taken his time.

2. A huge crowd came to the show, _____ the dreadful wind and rain.

3. The traffic jams held up so many fans on the way to the match, _____ the organisers delayed the kick-off by 30 minutes.

4. First they sang together, _____ they took turns to sing solos.

5. It is very cold and snowy _____ I still want to go out for a walk.

6. Harry really loved skateboarding _____ his twin brother Henry hated it.

■ Now use the remaining connectives to write six sentences of your own.

_____

_____

_____

_____

_____

_____

_____

_____

_____

Name:

Making connectives

■ Put two or more shorter words together to make a connective (for example, how + ever = however).

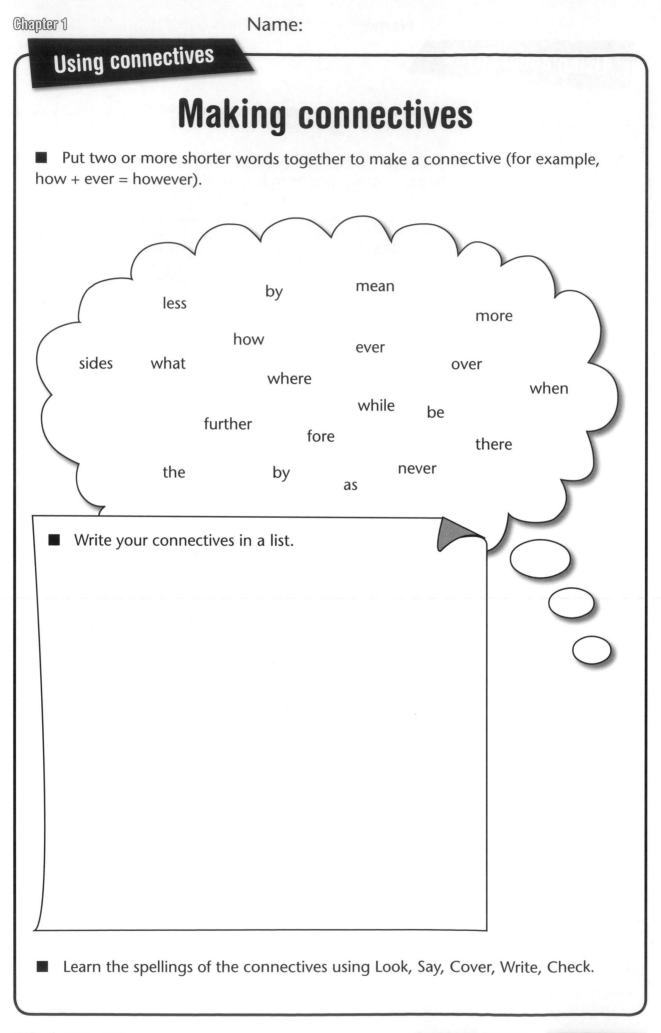

less   by   mean

more

how   ever

sides   what   over

where   when

while   be

further   fore   there

the   by   never

as

■ Write your connectives in a list.

■ Learn the spellings of the connectives using Look, Say, Cover, Write, Check.

PHOTOCOPIABLE

Using connectives

Tricky connectives

■ There are some mistakes in the spelling of the connectives in this paragraph. Draw a line through the incorrect connectives and rewrite them correctly in the box below.

> Our family just cannot decide where to go on holiday. Dad wants to go to a theme park, wheras Mum wants to go to the seaside. Morover she says she won't go to a theme park sinse theme parks make her feel sick! Berti and I will go anywhere, allthough I really like the idea of a theme park. Berti doesn't mind at all. Beesides, he will enjoy whattever we do sinse he is only a baby. Meanwile we keep arguing and conserquently everyone is in a bad mood. Therfour we are going to toss a coin and go where the coin lands. Alternativly, we just stay at home!

■ Now learn these connectives using Look, Say, Cover, Write, Check.

Look, Say and Cover	Write	Check
furthermore		
whereas		
since		
alternatively		
therefore		
although		
whatever		
meanwhile		
consequently		
moreover		
nonetheless		
besides		

Assessment

The following grid shows the main objectives and activities covered in this chapter. You can use the grid to locate activities that cover a particular focus that you are keen to monitor.

Objective	Page	Activity title
To investigate the addition of prefixes to root words as an aid to spelling using 'dis-', 'in-', 'im-', 'il-', 'ir-', 'un-' and 'mis-'.	13 14 15	Which negative prefix? Opposite sentences Prefix search
To use root words and suffixes '-ible', '-able', '-cian', '-sion', '-tion' as an aid to spelling.	17 18 19	i or a? Spot the imposters Which shun?
To investigate the spellings of connectives.	21 22 23	Connecting sentences Making connectives Tricky connectives

Observation and record keeping

Help the children to keep spelling journals. A note of rules, patterns and mnemonics will be helpful. Ensure that they reinforce the correct spelling. You can use spelling journals to provide evidence for assessing ongoing work.

● **Prefixes:** Watch out for children who alter the root word when adding a prefix, particularly when the prefix creates a double letter.

● **Suffixes:** Exposure to words which use the suffixes '-ible' and '-able' is the simplest way to help children learn which to use. When adding a vowel suffix to a word ending in 'e', we usually drop the final 'e'. Exceptions are soft 'g' (/j/), soft 'c' (/s/) or 's' (/s/) – for example, *changeable*. Words ending '-tion', '-sion', '-cian' are often verbs or adjectives converted to nouns (for example, *confuse/confusion*). Tell the children to look at the last consonant for a clue (for example, *congratulate – congratulations*).

● **Connectives:** Encourage the children to try using different connectives and explore how the meaning of the sentences alter.

Assessment activity

● **What you need**
Photocopiable page 25 'Creating and classifying' for each child, writing materials.

● **What to do**
Challenge the children to make as many new words as they can by adding one or more of the suffixes and/or prefixes to the root words and combining words to make connectives. Ask them to write their new words into the correct column. Finally, ask them to choose six words, turn their page over and write a paragraph that includes each of their chosen words.

Differentiation

● Remind and reinforce the spelling patterns orally with less confident spellers before beginning the activity. Write the words on individual cards so that the children can physically manipulate them, trying out different combinations before they choose a word.

● Extend more confident spellers by whiting-out the suffixes and prefixes. Explain that they need to decide which words to use with a prefix, and/or a suffix.

Further learning

● **Patterns:** Encourage the children to think carefully about these spelling patterns and rules when reading and writing in other areas of the curriculum.

● **Reading:** Ask the children to collect examples of any exceptions they find in their own reading.

● **Writing:** Provide the children with a list of six of the words from the previous photocopiable activities and challenge them to write them into a paragraph or a sentence.

Assessment

Creating and classifying

■ Use the words from the table to make new words. Write them in the correct columns. Then turn your page over and use six of the words in a paragraph.

Nouns	Adjectives	Connectives

organise	rational	im
magic	electric	un
replace	love	sion
opt	practical	tion
consider	active	dis
music	tasteful	ir
heartened	decide	cian
significant	response	ible
extend	reason	in
invite	accept	able
respective	patient	mis
ever	while	as
the	over	ever
more	who	what
mean	when	where
none	less	never
some	how	further

■ SCHOLASTIC
www.scholastic.co.uk   **PHOTOCOPIABLE**   Scholastic Literacy Skills
Spelling: Year 6   25

Chapter 2
Word families, roots and origins

Introduction

This chapter focuses on word families, prefixes and suffixes from Greek and Latin, and words that originate from French and Italian. Identifying common roots and word patterns is a powerful aid to spelling, providing children with good prediction skills.

The children are encouraged throughout the chapter to investigate word meanings, using dictionaries and encyclopedias. Investigations through personal reading and dictionaries are an important part of this work.

In this chapter

Word families page 28	To identify word roots, derivations and spelling patterns.
Greek and Latin words page 32	To use word roots with prefixes and suffixes that originate from Greek and Latin words.
Borrowed words page 36	To investigate the use of words that originated in other parts of the world.
Assessment page 40	Activities and ideas to assess knowledge of word families, roots and origins.

Poster notes

Words around the world (page 27)
This poster illustrates that English is a living, growing language and that English borrows words from other countries around the world. The poster contains pairs of words taken from other languages.

Display the poster and encourage the children to add 'borrowed' words they encounter in their own reading to the groups according to the country of origin. Place the poster on a large piece of paper, so that the children can also add new groups when they find words from other countries.

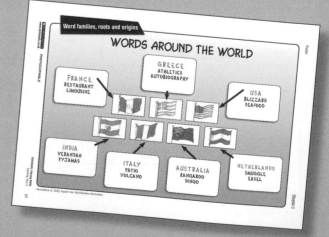

WORDS AROUND THE WORLD

Word families, roots and origins

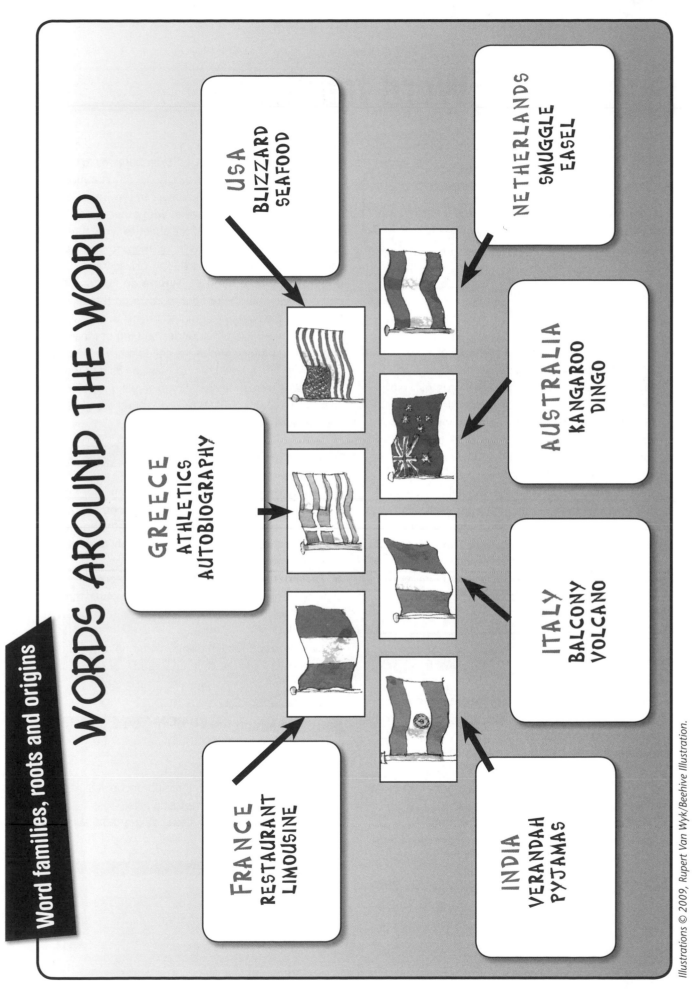

USA
BLIZZARD
SEAFOOD

NETHERLANDS
SMUGGLE
EASEL

GREECE
ATHLETICS
AUTOBIOGRAPHY

AUSTRALIA
KANGAROO
DINGO

FRANCE
RESTAURANT
LIMOUSINE

ITALY
BALCONY
VOLCANO

INDIA
VERANDAH
PYJAMAS

Illustrations © 2009, Rupert Van Wyk/Beehive Illustration.

Word families

Objective

To identify word roots, derivations and spelling patterns.

Background knowledge

A root word is a word or part of a word to which prefixes and suffixes can be added to make new words from the same word family. Knowledge of the spellings and meanings of root words will help children to spell and understand extended words within a word family. For example, knowing the root word *mobile* (meaning *movable*) will help children to spell other words in the same family: *mobility, mobilise, mobilisation, immobile, immobility*.

Knowledge of word families can help children to remember silent letters when they are sounded in certain word families (for example, *sign, signature, bomb, bombastic*), and unstressed vowels (*finite, definite*). Brainstorming and collecting words with the same root and grouping them into word families can help children to work out the meanings of the root words for themselves.

Activities

● **Photocopiable page 29 'Spidergram families'**
Children are given five root words, each in the centre of a spidergram. As they use a dictionary to investigate the root words they become familiar with the spelling patterns associated with the root words. Challenge them to use a dictionary to investigate further by finding prefixes that can be added to the root word.

● **Photocopiable page 30 'Letter strings'**
In this activity the children will be linking words derived from the root words and then underlining the common letter strings that remain consistent throughout the family. Draw the children's attention to the spelling

patterns that they notice. Ask: *What happens to some words when a suffix is added?* Discuss any common patterns that the children notice – can they make any general rules? Try out their rules with other words. Now ask them to use the back of the sheet to write the words into their family groups. Challenge them to practise spelling the words, using Look, Say, Cover, Write, Check.

● **Photocopiable page 31 'Where do I belong?'**
In this activity the children put words from the same family into the correct column according to their word class, thus reinforcing their understanding of meaning and spelling pattern. When the children have completed the activity, encourage them to make a chain of word families in a plenary session. For example, provide one child with a root word and then go round the group, adding words from the same family.

Further ideas

● **Family groups:** Make sets of word cards for families of words. Distribute them at random among the children in the class. Then ask the children to find their own families by checking other word cards until the children have all moved into different groups.

● **Personal collections:** As the children engage in personal reading, ask them to add the words they meet that are derived from root words to their personal word banks.

● **Daily roots:** Create a display with one root word a day and encourage the children to add words that are derived from it to the display using sticky notes.

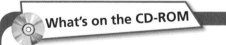 What's on the CD-ROM

On the CD-ROM you will find:
● Printable versions of all three photocopiable pages.
● Answers to all three photocopiable pages.
● Interactive versions of 'Letter strings' and 'Where do I belong?'.

Word families

Spidergram families

■ Look at the root word in these spidergrams. Add new words in the same word family to the arms. You can use a dictionary to help you.

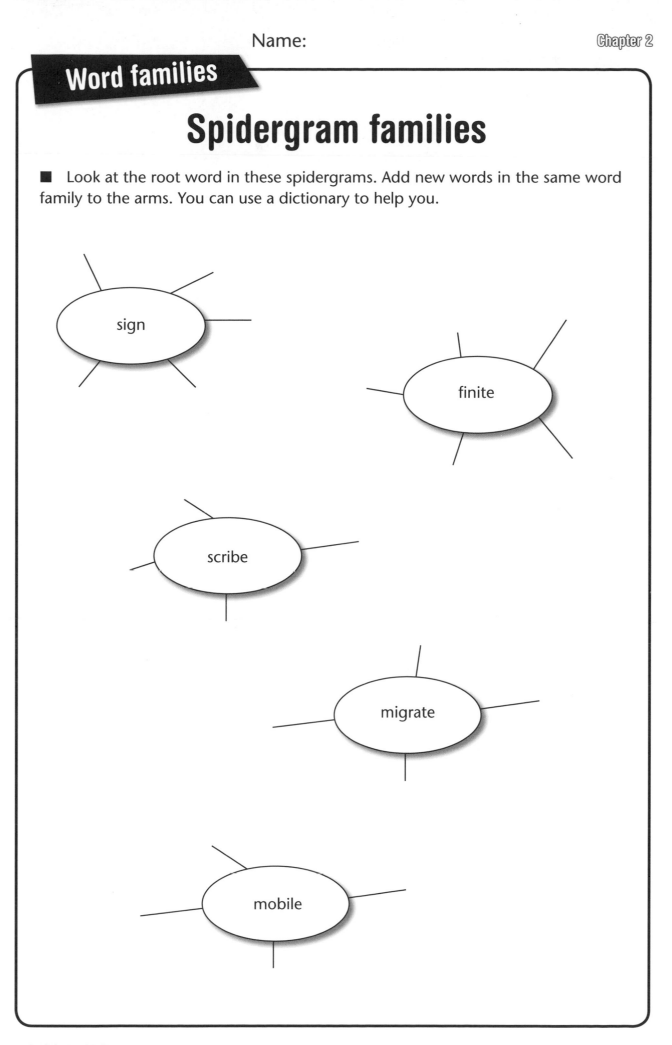

Name:

Word families

Letter strings

■ Draw lines to link the root words the other words in their word family. Underline the letter strings that remain the same for all words in each word family. The first one has been done for you.

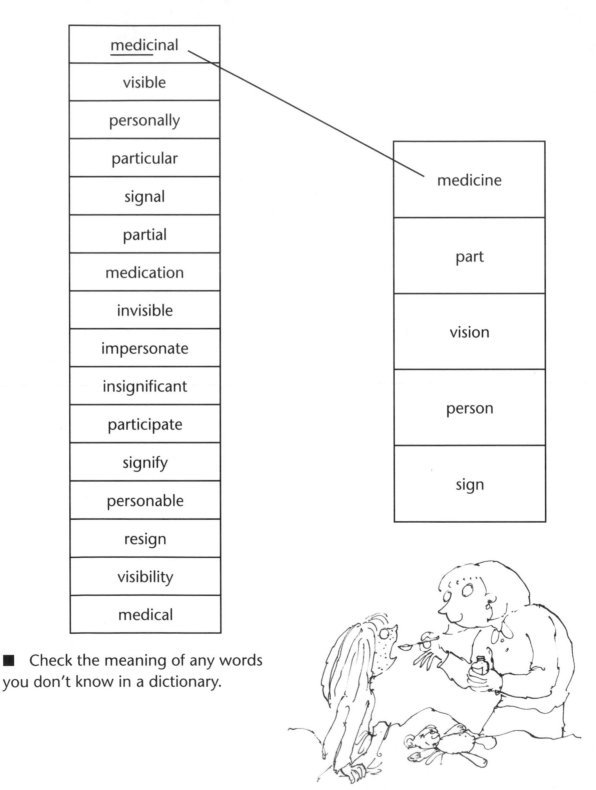

<u>medic</u>inal
visible
personally
particular
signal
partial
medication
invisible
impersonate
insignificant
participate
signify
personable
resign
visibility
medical

medicine
part
vision
person
sign

■ Check the meaning of any words you don't know in a dictionary.

PHOTOCOPIABLE

SCHOLASTIC
www.scholastic.co.uk

Illustrations © 2009, Rupert Van Wyk/Beehive Illustration.

Word families

Where do I belong?

■ Put the words on the page into the correct column to create word families.
Add any other words you know in the same family to the correct columns.

Verb	Noun	Person
break		
		builder
	painting	
create		
		survivor
plan		
explore		
	speech	
		assistant

speaker
breakage
exploration
plan
build
creator
paint
speak
assistance
painter
creation
survival
planner
breaker
explorer
assist
building
survive

Illustration © 2009, Rupert Van Wyk/Beehive Illustration.

Greek and Latin words

Objective

To use word roots with prefixes and suffixes that originate from Greek and Latin words.

Background knowledge

English spelling borrows words, prefixes and suffixes from other languages including Latin and Greek. An understanding of the meaning of Greek and Latin prefixes will help children to spell many words in English. For example, many words that begin with or contain the grapheme 'ph' are words that came from the Greek language. Knowing that many words have the Latin root *bene* (which means *well*) will help the children to recognise that several words such as *benefit, benevolent* and *benefactor* are spelled with a second 'e' which may be pronounced differently.

Activities

● **Photocopiable page 33 'Greek and Latin roots'**
Discuss the Greek and Latin root words listed on the photocopiable sheet with the children. Before handing out copies, ask the children to guess the meanings of the roots and suggest some words that might contain them. Check their ideas against the words and definitions on the sheet. Invite the children to complete the activities on the sheet, using dictionaries to check their work. As they explore the dictionary definition, they will find similar words with the same roots and reinforce their knowledge of the meaning of the Greek and Latin roots, leading to a wider vocabulary.

● **Photocopiable page 34 'Prefixes and suffixes'**
In this activity the children experiment with joining a Greek or Latin prefix to a Greek or Latin suffix to create new words. Encourage them to check their new words with a dictionary and practise spelling them using Look, Say, Cover, Write, Check. Follow up the activity by playing a game with the whole class or a large group. Create prefix/suffix cards and provide each child with a card. The children need to find someone with a card that can be combined with theirs to make a word. For a further challenge, encourage the children to create imaginary words using one or more of the Greek and Latin roots. Can they also make up definitions for their imaginary words?

● **Photocopiable page 35 'Number prefixes'**
This activity introduces the children to prefixes commonly used to denote number when associated with other nouns, adjectives and adverbs. Remind the children that they will find it easier to work out the definitions of the words if they look for common letter strings in the words. Suggest that they underline the chunks of the words that they think will help them to work out the meanings.

Further ideas

● **Shared and independent reading:** Suggest that the children collect other examples of words with Greek and Latin origins as they read.
● **Other curriculum areas:** Encourage the children to collect words with Greek and Latin origins from work in other areas of the curriculum (for example, numeracy, geography and science).

What's on the CD-ROM

On the CD-ROM you will find:
● Printable versions of all three photocopiable pages.
● Answers to 'Greek and Latin roots' and 'Prefixes and suffixes'.
● Interactive version of 'Prefixes and suffixes'.

Greek and Latin words

Greek and Latin roots

■ Look at these Greek and Latin roots.

Greek root	Meaning
chronos	time
autos	self
mikros	small
logos	study, speech
astron	star
graphein	to write
phone	sound

Latin root	Meaning
aqua	water
audire	hear
bene	good, well
spectare	look
facere	to do, to make

■ Underline the part or parts of these words that have a Greek or Latin origin. Write your own definition of each word then check it with a dictionary.

aquarium _____

chronological _____

audible _____

spectator _____

astronaut _____

facilitate _____

benefit _____

automatic _____

microphone _____

factory _____

Illustration © 2009, Rupert Van Wyk/Beehive Illustration.

Name:

Greek and Latin words

Prefixes and suffixes

■ Put these prefixes and suffixes together to make complete words. How many can you make?

■ Write them as a list at the bottom of the page. Check them in a dictionary and then practise spelling them using Look, Say, Cover, Write, Check.

Prefix	Suffix
photo	logy
bio	graph
auto	phone
micro	scope
hemi	sphere
mono	graphy
tele	matic

Word list

PHOTOCOPIABLE   ■SCHOLASTIC
www.scholastic.co.uk

Greek and Latin words

Number prefixes

■ We use Greek and Latin prefixes for adjectives, adverbs and nouns relating to numbers. For example, the Latin prefix **bi** means 'two' as in *bicycle* – a cycle with two wheels.

■ If you understand the meaning of the prefix it can help you to spell the word.

Prefix	Meaning	Origin
hemi	half	Greek
semi	half	Latin
uni	one	Latin
mono	one	Greek
bi	two	Latin
di	two	Greek
du	two	Latin
tri	three	Latin and Greek
quad	four	Latin
quart	four	Latin
quin	five	Latin
penta	five	Greek
hex	six	Greek
sex	six	Latin
hept	seven	Greek
oct	eight	Latin and Greek
non	nine	Latin
dec	ten	Latin and Greek
cent	hundred	Latin
mill	thousand	Latin

■ Find out what the following words mean. Write their definitions on a piece of paper. Check your answers in a dictionary.

decathlon	monologue	duplicate
hemisphere	biennial	unique
quarterly	triplicate	quintet
millennium	quadrilateral	sextet
pentangle	hexagon	septet
semicircle	nonagenarian	heptathlon
dialogue	centipede	octagon

Borrowed words

Objective

To investigate the use of words that originated in other parts of the world.

Background knowledge

English is a living and changing language that borrows many words from other languages and often retains the spelling patterns of those languages. To encourage children to take an active interest in words and their meanings, ask them to collect unusual and interesting words and use an etymological dictionary or encyclopedia to find out more about them and learn their use and spelling.

Activities

● **Photocopiable page 37 'Imported words'**
In this activity the children use a dictionary or encyclopedia to research the origins of words from around the world and write them onto a map to show which part of the world they come from. Before beginning the activity, read some of the words to the children and ask them if they are English words. Explain that we borrow words from around the world and encourage them to suggest such words from their own knowledge.

● **Photocopiable page 38 'Italian doubles'**
In this activity the children use a dictionary or encyclopedia to find the plural form and meaning of words that originate from Italian (all the words have double consonants). This provides children with the opportunity to learn how plurals are formed in words that end in vowels other than 'e'. English words do not commonly end in 'a' or 'i'.

● **Photocopiable page 39 'French'**
In this activity the children use a pronunciation guide to read and say aloud words that are borrowed from French. They write their own definitions and then check them with a dictionary. Before giving the children the photocopiable sheet, ask them if they know any French words. Suggest one for them (for example, *boutique*) and spend a few moments brainstorming others from their own knowledge.

Further ideas

● **Personal dictionaries:** Children can create their own etymological dictionaries for words with origins other than English.
● **On the lookout:** As the class shares a text, challenge them to look out for words from around the world.
● **Unusual plurals:** Make a class collection of words with unusual plural forms.

 ## What's on the CD-ROM

On the CD-ROM you will find:
● Printable versions of all three photocopiable pages.
● Answers to 'Italian doubles'.
● Interactive version of 'Imported words'.

Name:

Borrowed words

Imported words

■ Use an etymological dictionary or an encyclopedia to explore the origins of these words. Draw arrows from them to the right part of the world.

boomerang	chauffeur	easel
burger	cello	hoist
bungalow	dingo	igloo

kiwi	pizza	smuggle
macaroni	patio	toboggan
moccasins	restaurant	yacht

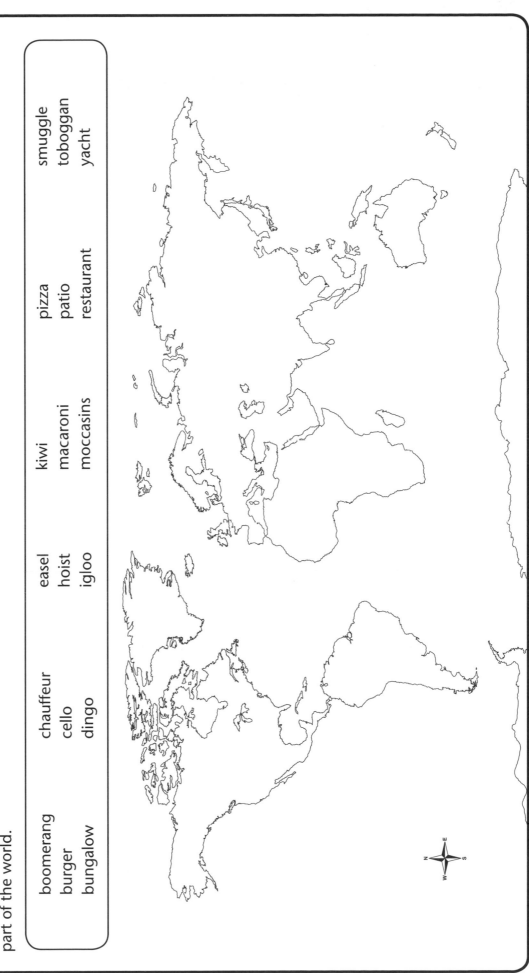

Illustration © 2009, The Drawing Room.

Name:

Borrowed words

Italian doubles

■ Use a dictionary to look up these words of Italian origin. Write the plural in the next column and the meaning in the last column. Be careful – some are already a plural form!

Word	Plural	Meaning
broccoli		
umbrella		
spaghetti		
regatta		
pizza		
graffiti		
ballot		
corridor		

■ Double letters can be confusing! Practise spelling the words using Look, Say, Cover, Write, Check.

Illustrations © 2009, Rupert Van Wyk/Beehive Illustration.

PHOTOCOPIABLE

■SCHOLASTIC
www.scholastic.co.uk

Borrowed words

French

■ We use many French words in English. Look at the list and say the words out loud. Then check your pronunciation with the guide.

■ Write your own definition of each word and then check them in a dictionary.

French words we use in English	Sounds like...	Definition
ballet	ballay	
camouflage	cam-er-flarge (with a soft **g** sound)	
debris	debree	
memoir	memwar (**ar** sounds like *car*)	
mortgage	more-gedge	
regime	rejeem (with a soft **g** sound)	
reservoir	reserve-war (**ar** sounds like *car*)	
sabotage	sab-er-targe (with a soft **g** sound)	
unique	you-neek	

■ Practise spelling these words using Look, Say, Cover, Write, Check.

Assessment

Assessment grid

The following grid shows the main objectives and activities covered in this chapter. You can use the grid to locate activities that cover a particular focus that you are keen to monitor.

Objective	Page	Activity title
To identify word roots, derivations and spelling patterns.	29 30 31	Spidergram families Letter strings Where do I belong?
To use word roots with prefixes and suffixes that originate from Greek and Latin words.	33 34 35	Greek and Latin roots Prefixes and suffixes Number prefixes
To investigate the use of words that originated in other parts of the world.	37 38 39	Imported words Italian doubles French

Observation and record keeping

● **Roots, derivations and spelling patterns**
Watch out for children who alter the spelling of the root word when adding a prefix, particularly when the added prefix creates a double letter. Learning the meaning and spelling patterns of Greek and Latin prefixes and suffixes will help children to avoid common spelling mistakes. For example, knowing the sound and spelling of the prefix 'auto' will help children avoid writing *autamatic* instead of *automatic*.

While the children are completing the photocopiable sheets in this chapter, encourage them to keep a spelling journal – for example, recording how well they did and any difficulties they encountered. Encourage them to write down any words that were tricky for them and

any mistakes they made. A note of appropriate rules, patterns and mnemonics will also be helpful to them. Ensure they reinforce the correct spelling. You can use spelling journals to provide evidence for assessing ongoing work.

Assessment activity

● **What you need**
Photocopiable page 41 'Word building' for each child, A4 paper, writing materials.
● **What to do**
Provide each child with the photocopiable sheet, pens and paper. Ask them to work independently to answer each of the four sections. Before they begin, check that they have understood what is required of them in each section.

Differentiation

● Go through each section of the assessment activity orally with less confident learners before they attempt them independently.
● Extend more confident learners by asking them to add an extra word in the first three sections. Extend them further by limiting the time allowed to complete the assessment sheet.

Further learning

● **Games:** Encourage the children to invent games such as finding tricky parts, creating word art, noting short words in long words, building words letter by letter, mnemonics, chunking words and saying them in unusual ways to help reinforce their learning.
● **Greek or Latin:** Encourage the children to think carefully about words with Greek or Latin prefixes and suffixes when reading and writing in other areas of the curriculum.
● **Writing:** Provide the children with a list of six of the words from the photocopiable sheets and challenge them to write them into a paragraph or a sentence.

Assessment

Word building

■ Write a word that begins with each of these prefixes.

audi _____   auto _____

bi _____   micro _____

hemi _____   aqua _____

tri _____   bene _____

■ Write a word that ends with each of these suffixes.

graphy _____   logy _____

phone _____   matic _____

■ Write two or three more words that are in the same word family for each of these words.

sign _____

finite _____

person _____

scribe _____

■ On a piece of paper, copy these words and write the name of its country of origin.

spaghetti	graffiti
chauffeur	camouflage
yacht	reservoir
escalator	unique

Illustration © 2009, Rupert Van Wyk/Beehive Illustration.

Chapter 3
Inflectional endings and terminology

Introduction

In this chapter you will find activities that focus on the use and understanding of inflectional endings and how understanding common patterns can help to develop spelling skills. Also, in this chapter you will find activities that involve using and understanding the terminology used to describe words and spellings (such as *homophone*, *antonym* and *mnemonic*).

Finally, you will find activities that concentrate on changing nouns to verbs and verbs to nouns using prefixes and suffixes, once more enhancing the children's understanding of the way things are spelled and how we can often predict the spelling of a word if we understand what it means.

In this chapter

Inflections and rules page 44	To spell words with inflectional endings '-ed' and '-ing', '-er' and '-est' for words ending in 'e' or 'y'. To invent own rules for pluralising nouns.
Terminology page 48	To become familiar with the meaning and use of terms used to talk about spelling and language.
Transforming words page 52	To extend work using suffixes and prefixes by changing nouns to verbs and verbs to nouns.
Assessment page 56	Activities and ideas to assess knowledge of inflectional endings and terminology.

Poster notes

Homophones (page 43)
This poster provides a list of homophones and will support the children's knowledge and work in language words and special terms. When introducing the poster to the children, mask the second and third words and ask the children to think of another word that sounds the same but has a different meaning and spelling. Reveal the homophones one by one. Encourage the children to add more homophones as they encounter new ones in their personal reading.

Inflectional endings and terminology

Homophones

brake break	bare bear	aloud allowed
days daze	check cheque	caught court
doe dough	die dye	dew due
flour flower	flew flu flue	ewe you yew
hear here	hair hare	genes jeans
knight night	knew new	hour our
medal meddle	made maid	knot not
peace piece	pair pare pear	muscle mussel
right rite write	rain reign rein	plain plane
seas sees seize	saw soar sore	rode rowed
stair stare	sight site	sew so sow
their there they're	steal steel	stationary stationery
vain vane vein	to too two	threw through
weather whether	wear where	weak week
	wood would	witch which

SCHOLASTIC
www.scholastic.co.uk   PHOTOCOPIABLE

Inflections and rules

To spell words with inflectional endings '-ed' and '-ing', '-er' and '-est' for words ending in 'e' or 'y'. To invent own rules for pluralising nouns.

Background knowledge

Inflectional endings are suffixes that, when added to root words, alter the case, number, meaning or tense. These suffixes have no lexical meaning on their own. Care needs to be taken when adding a vowel suffix to a root word that ends in 'e' or 'y'. Children need to be taught that words ending in 'y' drop the 'y' when adding '-ed', '-er' and '-est' and replace it with 'i'. They also need to be taught that words ending in 'y' keep the 'y' when adding '-ing'.

Activities

● **Photocopiable page 45 'Crossword'**
The children are given single word (verb) clues to help them fill in a crossword. They have to choose between the past tense '-ed' ending or the continuous '-ing' ending for verbs ending 'e' or 'y' (except for *dash* and *go*). They will find counting letters will help them to work out which ending to use. In a plenary session, ask the children to talk about what spelling patterns they noticed in these words when the suffixes were added. Together, generate a spelling rule for adding these endings. Find some further examples that conform to the rule you have made. Can the children find any exceptions?

● **Photocopiable page 46 'Comparisons'**
As the children add the suffixes '-er' and '-est' to adjectives ending in 'y' to form comparatives and superlatives, they reinforce the rule of dropping the final 'y' when adding a vowel suffix.

● **Photocopiable page 47 'Making plurals'**
In this activity the children change singular nouns into plural nouns and invent rules to help them remember how to pluralise nouns that end in 'y', and when to add '-es' and '-s'. Finally, challenge them to make irregular nouns into plurals. Together, think of some ways to remember these tricky words. Create a display poster of tricky plurals that the children may add to as they come across them.

Further ideas

● **Pelmanism:** Play a variation of this game. Create pairs of singular and plural noun word cards and ask the children to play with a partner. They must find pairs of cards (matching singular and plural nouns). They keep any matching pairs that they turn over.

● **Personal collections:** As the children engage in personal reading, ask them to collect words they meet that have unusual or tricky plural forms. Ask them to add words that drop 'y' when a suffix is added.

What's on the CD-ROM

On the CD-ROM you will find:
● Printable versions of all three photocopiable pages.
● Answers to all three photocopiable pages.
● Interactive versions of 'Crossword' and 'Comparisons'.

Inflections and rules

Crossword

■ Add **-ed** or **-ing** to the words in the clues below to fill in the crossword.

Across
1. take
4. sample
6. glare
9. dance
10. place
12. cry
16. deny
17. ignore
18. dash

Down
1. taste
2. go
3. glance
5. move
7. lie
8. rage
11. care
13. ignore
14. fly
15. cry

Illustration © 2009, Rupert Van Wyk/Beehive Illustration.

Name:

Inflections and rules

Comparisons

■ Add the suffixes **-er** and **-est** to the root words to show comparisons.

10 + 10 is an easy sum.

2 + 2 is an _____ sum.

1 + 1 is the _____ sum.

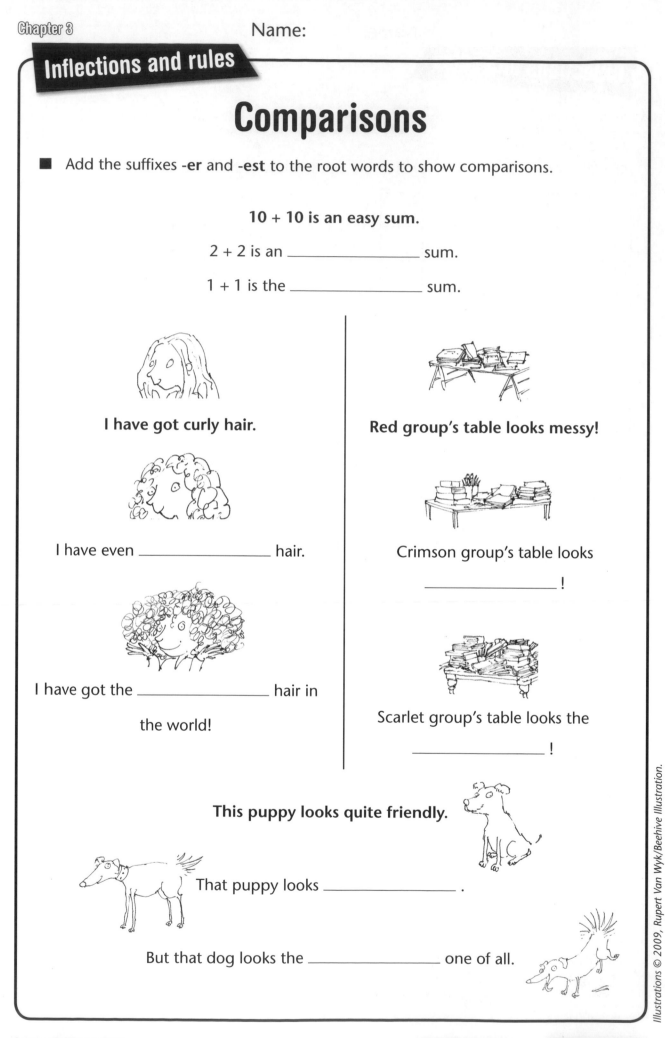

I have got curly hair.

I have even _____ hair.

I have got the _____ hair in

the world!

Red group's table looks messy!

Crimson group's table looks

_____ !

Scarlet group's table looks the

_____ !

This puppy looks quite friendly.

That puppy looks _____ .

But that dog looks the _____ one of all.

Illustrations © 2009, Rupert Van Wyk/Beehive Illustration.

PHOTOCOPIABLE

SCHOLASTIC
www.scholastic.co.uk

Inflections and rules

Making plurals

■ Change these nouns to plural nouns:

key becomes _____

daisy becomes _____

donkey becomes _____

family becomes _____

city becomes _____

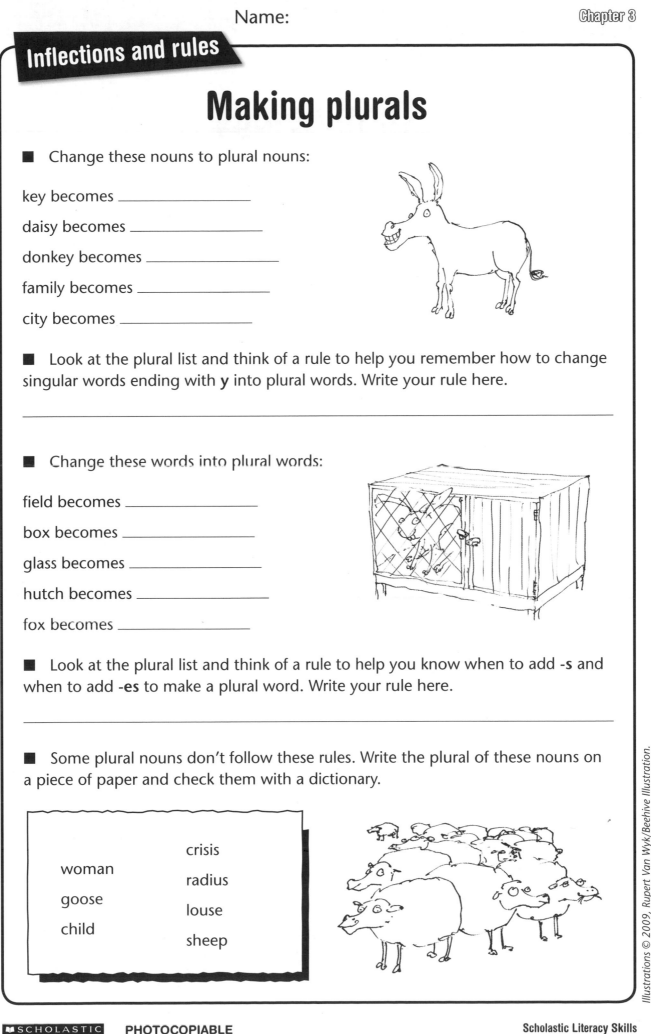

■ Look at the plural list and think of a rule to help you remember how to change singular words ending with **y** into plural words. Write your rule here.

_____

■ Change these words into plural words:

field becomes _____

box becomes _____

glass becomes _____

hutch becomes _____

fox becomes _____

■ Look at the plural list and think of a rule to help you know when to add **-s** and when to add **-es** to make a plural word. Write your rule here.

_____

■ Some plural nouns don't follow these rules. Write the plural of these nouns on a piece of paper and check them with a dictionary.

woman

goose

child

crisis

radius

louse

sheep

Illustrations © 2009, Rupert Van Wyk/Beehive Illustration.

Terminology

Objective

To become familiar with the meaning and use of terms used to talk about spelling and language.

Background knowledge

Specific words are used as terms to describe language and spelling, such as *noun*, *clause*, *phrase*, *phoneme*, *syllable* or *mnemonic*. Children should become familiar with their meanings and use so that discussion about the spelling of words and their use in writing is clear both to the children and to the teacher. Many of these terms have interesting and unusual spelling patterns. Encourage the children's interest in words and spelling oddities by drawing their attention to unusual letter use (for example, 'y' in *syllable*, *synonym*, *acronym* and *antonym*, the silent 'm' in *mnemonic* and so on).

Activities

● **Photocopiable page 49 'Language words'**
Introduce the activity by talking about how we use special vocabulary to talk about different aspects of life. For example, ask the children to describe some of their hobbies or pastimes and say words that relate specifically to them and are not often used outside of the hobby. Explain that this helps people who are involved in an activity to understand details about it. The children are given a list of words that are terms used when speaking about spelling and language. They write their own definition of the words and put them into a sentence, then check the definition with a dictionary. In a plenary session, ask the children to describe, using their own words, how understanding and using the language words will help them to learn how to spell them.

● **Photocopiable page 50 'Special terms'**
Children are given another set of terms used to describe language. As they decide which word is missing in the sentence they reinforce their knowledge about each of the terms and its use. Encourage the children to check their answers in a dictionary. Are they surprised by any of the definitions?

● **Photocopiable page 51 'Terminology grid'**
In the course of this activity, the children will have to answer clues or riddles to fill in the grid of terms used to describe language. This means that they will have to think carefully before deciding which term is the correct answer. As they complete the grid, they practise their spelling skills by using letters already in the grid from previous answers to work out which word fits. If a further challenge would be useful for some children, hide the word box before copying the page.

Further ideas

● **Synonyms and antonyms:** Hold a quiz where you say a word and challenge the children to say either a synonym or antonym for the word.

● **Word families:** Create a display of word groups. For example: words about the alphabet; words about sound; word classes; words about meaning. Encourage children to add to the display using words on sticky notes.

● **Word of the day:** Choose a term about spelling, words and language each day and encourage children to use it in a sentence during the day.

What's on the CD-ROM

On the CD-ROM you will find:
● Printable versions of all three photocopiable pages.
● Answers to 'Special terms' and 'Terminology grid'.
● Interactive versions of 'Special terms' and 'Terminology grid'.

Name:

Terminology

Language words

■ We use special terms to describe letters and words. Write down your definition for each of the words in the table below. Then write a sentence with the word in it. Check your definition with a dictionary.

Term	Meaning	Sentence
vowel		
sentence		
clause		
phrase		
hyphen		
syllable		
verb		
noun		
adverb		
adjective		

■ Investigate these other words and write your definitions and sentences on a piece of paper.

| preposition | connective | apostrophe | consonant | segment |
| pronoun | ellipsis | paragraph | phoneme | blend |

■SCHOLASTIC
www.scholastic.co.uk

PHOTOCOPIABLE

Name:

Terminology

Special terms

■ Use the terms listed below to complete the sentences. Check your answers with a dictionary.

syllables	synonym	consonants	suffix	homonyms
homophones	antonym	prefix	acronym	mnemonic

1. We add the _____ **un** to make a word with the opposite meaning.

2. A word with the opposite meaning is an _____ .

3. There are 21_____ in the alphabet.

4. The _____ *asap* means 'as soon as possible'.

5. There are three _____ in the word *homonym*.

6. I use the _____ 'The knight is the king's brother' to help me remember how to spell *knight*.

7. *Break* and *brake*, which sound the same but have different spellings, are called _____ .

8. A _____ for *confused* might be *muddled*.

9. 'Biology' means the study of life and is made by putting together the prefix **bio** (life) with the _____ **logy** (study).

10. Two words with the identical sound and spelling but different meanings are called _____ . For example, the verb *catch* (get hold of) and the noun *catch* (a problem).

Illustrations © 2009, Rupert Van Wyk/Beehive Illustration.

PHOTOCOPIABLE

SCHOLASTIC
www.scholastic.co.uk

Name:

Terminology grid

Fill in the word grid by answering the clues. Find the right word from the word box below. The first one has already been done as an example.

Word box: exclamation, verb, sentence, noun, prefix, adjective, synonym, acronym, clause, adverb, passive, mnemonic, consonant

Across

1. My first syllable is in Sylvia. My next is in Stella. My last is in table.
2. I could be a name, place or thing and I rhyme with clown.
3. A punctuation mark for emphasis.
8. My first syllable is in constant. My next is in sonata. My last is in pleasant.
10. You cannot write a sentence without me.
11. Rhymes with massive.
12. My first syllable is in across. My next is in wrong. My last is in nymph.

Down

1. My first syllable rhymes with men. My last sounds like tense.
4. A homophone for the sharp bits on an animal's paws.
5. I am used with verbs to describe how something is done. My last syllable rhymes with herb.
6. My first syllable is in admire. My next is in object. My last is in relative.
7. Rhymes with demonic.
9. I am a word that is similar to another word and my last syllable rhymes with hymn.
11. I am a word that sounds like it could mean 'before mend'.

1. s y l l a b l e

SCHOLASTIC
www.scholastic.co.uk
PHOTOCOPIABLE

Transforming words

Objective

To extend work using suffixes and prefixes by changing nouns to verbs and verbs to nouns.

Background knowledge

A root word is a word or part of a word to which prefixes and suffixes can be added to make new words from the same word family. Knowledge of the spellings and meanings of root words will help children to spell and understand extended words within a word family. The suffixes that are used in this chapter to change verbs to nouns are: '-tion', '-sion', '-ment', '-ance', '-age', '-al' and '-ture'. There are few sure rules for adding these suffixes. Exposure to the root verbs and their respective nouns will help children learn how the suffix addition affects the spelling of the root – for example, when adding the suffix '-ure' to *fail*, just add it. However the spelling of *furnish* needs to be changed and *sign* requires an extra 'a' added before 'ture'.

Some general rules that can help children are:
- verbs ending in '-ck' usually add the suffix '-age';
- verbs ending in '-de' usually add the suffix '-sion'.

The most effective way to teach children the spelling patterns is by exposure and use. When they become familiar with the words they can ask themselves: *Does it sound right?*

Activities

- **Photocopiable page 53 'Verbs to nouns'**
The children are given a list of verbs and seven suffixes that are commonly used to transform verbs into nouns. As they write the nouns into the correct suffix box, encourage them to say the words out loud and think: *Does it sound right?* Further consolidation of the correct suffix use occurs when the children use a dictionary and investigate how to use the nouns in a sentence of their own on the back of the photocopiable sheet.

- **Photocopiable page 54 'Nouns to verbs'**
The children are given ten sentences that include a noun made by adding a suffix. As they investigate the noun to establish the root word, they will be breaking up the word into root and suffix and this will reinforce the spelling patterns of adding suffixes. By writing new sentences using the root word as a verb, they will be consolidating their understanding.

- **Photocopiable page 55 'Prefix patterns'**
As the children say out loud each of the nouns and experiment with adding the prefixes 'be-' and 'en-', they are encouraged to use probability to decide which is the correct prefix. Using a dictionary will enable them to check their knowledge of spelling and help them to understand the meaning of the word. Finally, using the words in sentences will contextualise the learning and make the spellings and their meanings more memorable.

Further ideas

- **Word cards:** Make cards of the prefixes, suffixes and verbs found in the activities on the photocopiable sheets. Encourage the children to join the cards together to change the verb into a noun.

What's on the CD-ROM

On the CD-ROM you will find:
- Printable versions of all three photocopiable pages.
- Answers to all three photocopiable pages.
- Interactive version of 'Prefix patterns'.

Transforming words

Verbs to nouns

■ Change the verbs in the list into nouns by writing the noun into the correct suffix box.

-tion	-ment	-ance

-age	-ure	-sion

to adjust	to endure	to maintain
to arrange	to erode	to modify
to arrive	to explode	to press
to block	to fail	to protrude
to break	to furnish	to sign
to conclude	to improve	to survive
to cultivate	to insure	to transform
to depart	to leak	to wreck

-al

Name:

Transforming words

Nouns to verbs

■ In each sentence there is a noun that has been made by adding a suffix to a verb. Underline the root word (verb) in each of these nouns and write a sentence of your own using the verb instead of the noun. Use a dictionary to help you and check that you have used the words as verbs and not adjectives in your sentences. The first one has already been done as an example.

1. When the tree reaches maturity it will be ten metres high.
   When I **mature** I might be 180cm tall.

2. Donald has a vivid imagination.

_____

3. Can you find the solution to the problem before the lesson ends?

_____

4. Make a shallow depression in the surface by lightly pushing with your thumb.

_____

5. Information retrieval is an important skill.

_____

6. Their laughter rang through the vast hall.

_____

7. The variation in temperature in this greenhouse ranges from 0 degrees to 40 degrees.

_____

8. When the pictures were printed, we all admired her photography.

_____

9. To my amazement we won, despite having fewer players on our team.

_____

10. To the best of my knowledge, he finished the game himself.

_____

PHOTOCOPIABLE ■SCHOLASTIC
www.scholastic.co.uk

Transforming words

Prefix patterns

■ These nouns can be changed into verbs by adding a prefix **be-** or **en-**. Say the words out loud with each prefix first. Does it sound right?

■ Now write the nouns into the correct box by adding the correct prefix.

■ On a piece of paper, write a sentence for each of the verbs, such as: *He woke up to find himself entangled in all the bedclothes.* Use a dictionary to help you.

act

circle

courage

danger

devil

friend

force

grudge

joy

moan

rage

siege

slave

tangle

trance

witch

be-

en-

Illustrations © 2009, Rupert Van Wyk/Beehive Illustration.

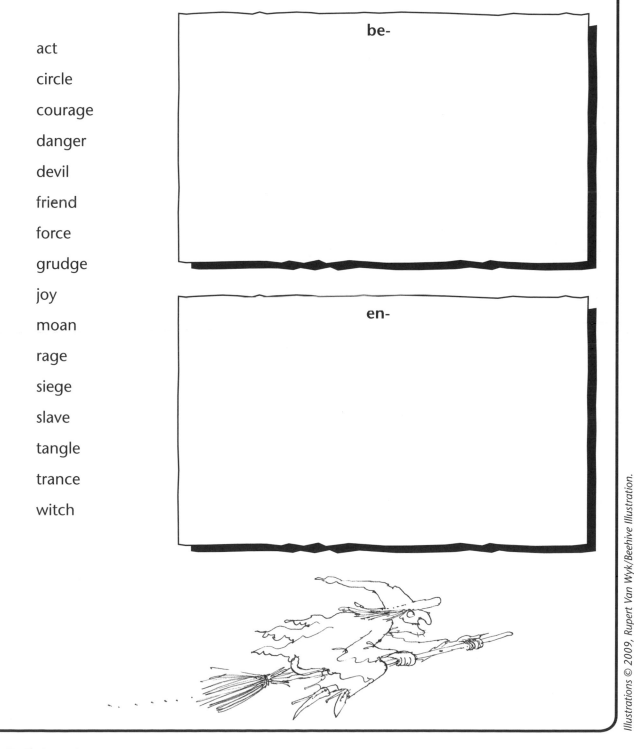

Assessment

The following grid shows the main objectives and activities covered in this chapter. You can use the grid to locate activities that cover a particular focus that you are keen to monitor.

Objective	Page	Activity title
To spell words with inflectional endings '-ed' and '-ing', '-er' and '-est' for words ending in 'e' or 'y'. To invent own rules for pluralising nouns.	45 46 47	Crossword Comparisons Making plurals
To become familiar with the meaning and use of terms used to talk about spelling and language.	49 50 51	Language words Special terms Terminology grid
To extend work using suffixes and prefixes by changing nouns to verbs and verbs to nouns.	53 54 55	Verbs to nouns Nouns to verbs Prefix patterns

Observation and record keeping

Most of the spellings in the assessment activity are revisiting words the children will have encountered during this chapter, but some are not. This gives you the opportunity to observe if the children really understand the conventions that were covered.

While the children are completing the activities in this chapter, encourage them to keep a spelling journal, for example, recording how well they did and any difficulties they encountered. Encourage them to write down any words that were tricky for them and any mistakes they made. A note of appropriate rules, patterns and mnemonics will also be helpful to them. Ensure that they reinforce the correct spelling.

For example:

Tricky words	I wrote	Tricky part	Correct spelling
denied	denyed	change the 'y' to 'i'	denied

Use spelling journals to provide evidence for assessing ongoing work.

Assessment activity

● **What you need**
Photocopiable page 57 'Missing words' for each child, writing materials.
● **What to do**
Provide each child with a copy of the photocopiable sheet. Ask them to write the missing word in each sentence, using the root words provided. Remind them to use all the spelling strategies available to them; suggest that they ask themselves: *Does the word look right? Does it follow a pattern or rule?*

Differentiation

● Go through each sentence of the assessment activity orally with less confident spellers, before they attempt the activity independently.
● Extend groups of more confident learners by masking the words given on the right-hand side of the page. Extend them further by limiting the time allowed to complete the assessment sheet.

Further learning

● **Technical terms:** When talking about spelling with the children, encourage them to use the terms that describe language, such as *syllable, phoneme, consonant* and *vowel*, in order that they become familiar with their meaning and use.

Assessment

Missing words

■ Fill in the missing words in each sentence using the root words provided.

1. Yesterday he _____ being at the scene despite the evidence. **deny**

2. That play was the _____ we have ever seen. **funny**

3. _____ grow in the summer. **daisy**

4. She sent 20 _____ to her friends. **invite**

5. A new haircut improved his _____ . **appear**

6. There has been a big _____ in their spelling. **improve**

7. All _____ must be paid for. **break**

8. The time of _____ will be announced later today. **depart**

9. The _____ to the argument is written at the bottom. **conclude**

10. Their _____ is threatened by climate change. **survive**

11. The ship was _____ in the middle of the sea. **calm**

12. They were _____ by an angry crowd. **circle**

Illustrations © 2009, Rupert Van Wyk/Beehive Illustration.

Chapter 4

Grouping and classifying

Introduction

This chapter focuses on learning spelling rules and their exceptions, inventing rules and mnemonics and learning polysyllabic words with unstressed vowels. It is important that children continue to be aware of the importance of root words when spelling words with unstressed vowels, along with their knowledge of suffixes. Throughout the chapter, children are encouraged to carry out investigations and record their findings in spelling journals. Using investigations can help children become more confident in their spelling abilities as it allows them to problem solve and makes them actively deconstruct words. It enables them to build confidence in their ability to solve spelling problems independently.

In this chapter

Rule or exception? page 60	To investigate and learn a range of spelling rules and their exceptions.
Unstressed vowels page 65	To investigate and learn the spellings of words with unstressed vowels.
Establishing rules page 70	To learn and invent a range of spelling rules.
Assessment page 74	Activities and ideas to assess knowledge of grouping and classifying.

Poster notes

Mnemonics (page 59)
This poster provides six examples of mnemonics for spelling the words *hear, rhythm, separate, necessary, accommodation* and *because*. Read the mnemonics aloud to the children, one at a time, using actions to accompany each mnemonic – for example, wriggle your hips (for *rhythm*) or draw the letters in the air. Having a visual as well as auditory impression will help children to remember the spellings. As they learn or invent their own mnemonics, encourage them to add them to the poster or wall to make a display.

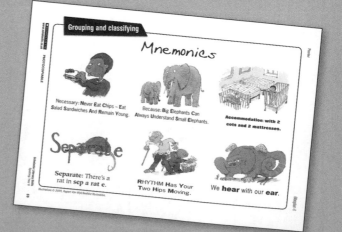

Mnemonics

Accommodation: with 2 cots and 2 mattresses.

We **hear** with our **ear**.

Because: **Big Elephants Can Always Understand Small Elephants**.

RHYTHM **Has Your Two Hips Moving**.

Necessary: **Never Eat Chips – Eat Salad Sandwiches And Remain Young**.

Separate: There's a rat in **sep a rat e**.

Grouping and classifying

Illustrations © 2009, Rupert Van Wyk/Beehive Illustration.

Rule or exception?

Objective

To investigate and learn a range of spelling rules and their exceptions.

Background knowledge

There are many rules to help children learn to spell. Learning these general rules draws their attention to their exceptions. Further investigation can help children discover the origins of words – for example, words in English do not normally end in 'i' but use 'y'. Exceptions include borrowed or imported words, such as *spaghetti*.

If children are encouraged to discover rules themselves through investigation, they will be much more likely to remember the rules and exceptions.

Activities

● **Photocopiable page 61 'Which /k/ am I?'**
Children are given a list of words that end either in 'ck', 'k' or 'c'. As they group the words according to their endings, they should become aware of the rule that the /k/ sound at the end of a word is spelled 'ck' when preceded by a single-syllable short vowel sound such as *clock*, 'k' when preceded by a single-syllable long vowel sound such as *week*, but 'c' in polysyllabic words such as *traumatic*.

● **Photocopiable page 62 'Changing y to i'**
In this activity the children will be adding suffixes to words ending in 'y'. Encourage them to think carefully about what happens to the root words as the suffixes are added. Ask them to generate a general rule and help them to notice that when a suffix is added to root words ending in 'y' preceded by a consonant, the 'y' changes to 'i' (*carried*), but the 'y' is kept before suffixes that begin with 'i'. Ask the children to note what happens to the word *buy* where the 'y' is preceded by a vowel. Can they find any other words that fit this pattern?

● **Photocopiable page 63 'Doubling consonants'**
As the children add suffixes to verbs with short or long vowel sounds, help them to understand the rule that single-syllable words with short vowel sounds double the consonant when adding a suffix; long vowel sounds do not.

● **Photocopiable page 64 'Which order?'**
Probably one of the most widely used spelling rules relating to vowels in words is the rule: *'i' before 'e' except after 'c'*. This rule has a number of exceptions which children need to learn. In this activity the children use a dictionary to add words to three columns: words that use the 'i' before 'e' pattern; words that use 'ei' following 'c'; words that are exceptions to the 'i' before 'e' rule. As they add words to each column, encourage them to find their own rule to explain the spelling patterns. Check that they are categorising the words in the correct way. Help the children to note that the rule applies when the sound in these words is /ee/ – where it is not /ee/ the rule has exceptions.

Further ideas

● **Shared and independent reading:** As the children read with the class and independently, encourage them to collect exceptions to known spelling rules.
● **Rule of the day:** Choose a spelling rule each day and challenge the children to add words which prove the rule.

What's on the CD-ROM

On the CD-ROM you will find:
● Printable versions of all four photocopiable pages.
● Answers to 'Which /k/ am I?', 'Changing y to i' and 'Doubling consonants'.
● Interactive versions of 'Which /k/ am I?' and 'Changing y to i'.

Rule or exception?

Which /k/ am I?

■ Look at the words below. Can you see a pattern or rule for words that end with the /k/ sound? Sort the words according to the three different spelling patterns and write your rule at the bottom of the page.

back	pack	seek	deck	horrific
meek	peck	stuck	terrific	ark
track	sonic	trick	fleck	automatic
traffic	luck	fantastic	dock	leak
flick	lock	park	lurk	prolific
knock	truck	lick	frolic	frantic

k endings	**c** endings	**ck** endings

■ Write your rule here.

_____

_____

■ Can you find any exceptions? Add the rule and exceptions to your spelling journal.

Name:

Rule or exception?

Changing y to i

■ Add the suffixes to each word and find the rule and the exception.

try + ed = _____

ing = _____

hurry + ed = _____

ing = _____

rely + ing = _____

able = _____

funny + er = _____

est = _____

merry + ment = _____

er = _____

stray + ed = _____

ing = _____

carry + er = _____

ing = _____

buy + er = _____

ing = _____

The rule is: _____

_____

It is a different rule when: _____

_____

■ Add the rule to your spelling journal.

PHOTOCOPIABLE   ■SCHOLASTIC
www.scholastic.co.uk

Rule or exception?

Doubling consonants

■ Add the suffixes to these words to find a rule about doubling consonants.

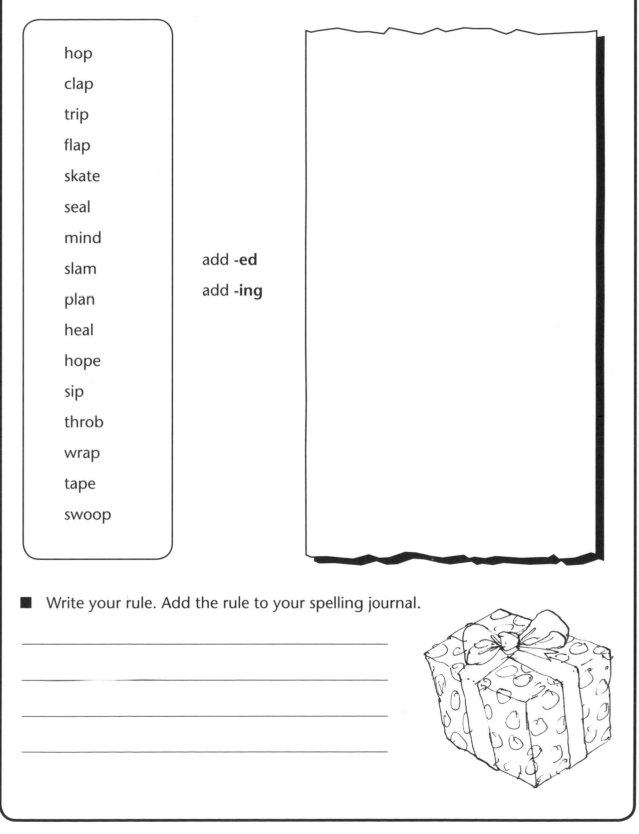

hop

clap

trip

flap

skate

seal

mind

slam

plan

heal

hope

sip

throb

wrap

tape

swoop

add **-ed**

add **-ing**

■ Write your rule. Add the rule to your spelling journal.

_____

_____

_____

_____

Illustrations © 2009, Rupert Van Wyk/Beehive Illustration.

■SCHOLASTIC
www.scholastic.co.uk   **PHOTOCOPIABLE**   **Scholastic Literacy Skills**
Spelling: Year 6 **63**

Name:

Rule or exception?

Which order?

■ Use a dictionary to find and add words with the letter strings **ie** and **ei** to these three columns. Compare the words you have written in the first and middle columns. What pattern can you find?

piece	ceiling	foreign
believe	receive	weird

■ Write the rule here. Add the rule and exceptions to your spelling journal.

_____

_____

PHOTOCOPIABLE   ■SCHOLASTIC
www.scholastic.co.uk

Unstressed vowels

Objective

To investigate and learn the spellings of words with unstressed vowels.

Background knowledge

There are many words with vowels that are difficult to hear because they are spoken quickly or quietly. When the stress falls on one syllable and not another, the vowel in the unstressed syllable is often unsounded when spoken. Common instances of unstressed vowels can be found in the suffixes '-ary' and '-ory'. Also the letter strings 'er' and 'ed' are frequently unstressed. It can be helpful to get the children to say the words aloud and sound the unstressed letters, for example, 'sep-a-rate'. Encourage the children also to deconstruct the words by breaking them into syllables, identifying prefixes and suffixes and words within words.

Activities

● **Photocopiable page 66 'Hidden vowels'**
In this activity the children copy a list of words and identify which vowels are unstressed. As they break each word up into chunks containing the vowel sounds, they say the words aloud to stress these vowels. Explain that some of the vowel sounds may be represented by vowel digraphs such as the 'oi' in *poisonous*. Make sure the children understand that they are not trying to break the word up into syllables.

● **Photocopiable page 67 'ary, ery or ory?'**
In this activity the children are encouraged to try out three different suffixes for each root word in a list. They will be relying on visual strategies (*Does it look right?*) to make their choice of spelling, crossing out the words that don't look right. Encourage them to identify the unstressed vowel and ask them to check their answers in a dictionary. Are there any particular patterns that will help the children remember the words? Invite them to make up a mnemonic for the word that they find the hardest to remember. Share all the children's ideas and display them.

● **Photocopiable page 68 'Missing vowels'**
The children are given a list of misspelled words with the unstressed vowel missed out. Ask them to predict the missing vowel before they use a dictionary to investigate. After the children have completed the activity, ask them to work with a partner, saying the words but stressing the unstressed vowels (saying it as it is spelled) to reinforce the spelling.

● **Photocopiable page 69 'Roots'**
Finish the work in this section with a fun crossword. Remind the children to watch out – all the answers to the clues are words with unstressed vowels. Once they have completed the crossword, ask the children to write the words on the back of the sheet and learn them using the Look, Say, Cover, Write, Check strategy.

Further ideas

● **Say it aloud:** Encourage the children to voice the unstressed vowels in words as they say them aloud.
● **Vowel patterns:** Ask the children to decorate written words for a class display, using colours and patterns for the unstressed vowels.
● **More choices:** Challenge the children to continue the work on '-ory', '-ary' or '-ery' by making choices for the following roots: *mission, explain, deliver, diction* and *revolution*. Ask them to include the new words in sentences to contextualise the learning.

What's on the CD-ROM

On the CD-ROM you will find:
● Printable versions of all four photocopiable pages.
● Answers to all four photocopiable pages.
● Interactive versions of 'ary, ery or ory?', 'Missing vowels' and 'Roots'.

Name:

Unstressed vowels

Hidden vowels

■ Copy each word and say it aloud. Underline any vowel that is unstressed. Then write each word into the boxes so that each box contains a vowel sound (including **y**). The first is done as an example.

library	library		lib	ra	ry	

general _____

different _____

poisonous _____

necessary _____

vocabulary _____

holiday _____

separate _____

fattening _____

signature _____

parliament _____

conference _____

■ Say the words out loud, exaggerating the vowel sounds in the boxes (for example, 'par-li-a-ment').

■ Now practise spelling them using Look, Say, Cover, Write, Check.

Illustration © 2009, Rupert Van Wyk/Beehive Illustration.

PHOTOCOPIABLE ■SCHOLASTIC www.scholastic.co.uk

Unstressed vowels

ary, ery or ory?

■ Add each suffix to the word stems. Which one looks right? Cross out the ones you think are wrong and underline the unstressed vowel. Then check with a dictionary.

	-ary	-ery	-ory
Janu			
Febru			
mem			
slipp			
fact			
thund			
constabul			
sal			
categ			
discov			
laborat			
*station			

*Be careful with this one – there are two correct words with different meanings!

■ Read your list of correct words aloud and stress the unstressed vowels. Now practise spelling the words using Look, Say, Cover, Write, Check.

Illustration © 2009, Rupert Van Wyk/Beehive Illustration.

Name:

Unstressed vowels

Missing vowels

■ The unstressed vowels have been left out of these words. Use a dictionary to help you find the missing vowels. Write the missing vowel in the next column and then rewrite the words correctly.

Incorrect	Missing vowel	Correct
necessry		
memrable		
confrence		
desprate		
compny		
refrence		
litrature		
revolutionry		
abandond		
boundry		
minature		
lemnade		
consnant		
histry		
frightning		
secretry		
vegtable		

PHOTOCOPIABLE

Unstressed vowels

Roots

■ Use the clues about root words at the bottom of the page to fill in the word grid. Take care – all the words contain unstressed vowels.

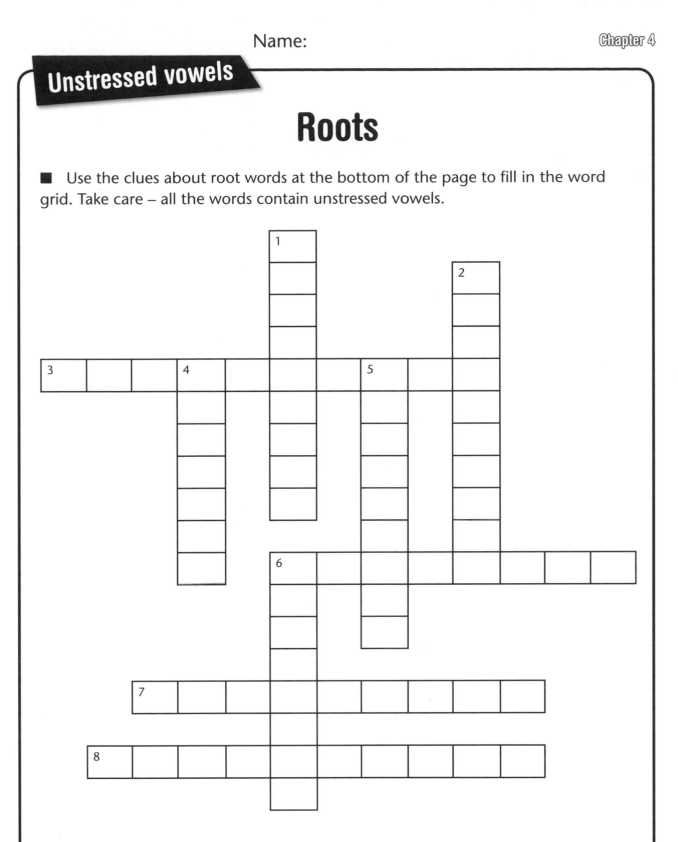

Across

3. This will occur when something differs.
6. Made to remain silent.
7. You can be this if you despair.
8. Was showing interest.

Down

1. This will refer to something.
2. What is the screen showing the vision called?
4. Things are manufactured here.
5. In nature, things happen like this.
6. You might slip on this sort of surface.

■ SCHOLASTIC   **PHOTOCOPIABLE**
www.scholastic.co.uk

Establishing rules

Objective

To learn and invent a range of spelling rules.

Background knowledge

There are many rules for spelling in English but most rules have exceptions. When teaching a rule to children they need to learn the exceptions. When children investigate spelling patterns and invent their own rules for spelling, they are more likely to remember the spelling patterns. It is important to stress that the children must understand their own rules and also be aware of exceptions. It can be useful to get the children to test their rule out on a partner to make sure it can be understood.

Activities

● **Photocopiable page 71 'Hard and soft c'**
In this activity the children find words written in an unbroken circle. Each word begins with the last letter of the previous word and contains either a hard or soft /c/ sound. As they rewrite the words into two boxes they discover a pattern for spelling these words – that the letter 'c' is soft when it comes before the vowels 'e' and 'i', and the letter 'c' is hard when it is followed by a consonant. If the activity is too challenging for some children, help them to get started by underlining or highlighting one of the complete words to give them a starting point. Tell them to sound the phonemes aloud and check that they have ended the word on the correct letter by listening to see if it makes sense and is a real word.

● **Photocopiable page 72 'Mnemonics'**
As the children look for shorter words within words, they invent their own mnemonics to help remember the spelling of tricky words. Looking for shorter words in longer words helps children's visual spelling strategies and creating their own mnemonics will further reinforce the strategy. After running the activity, hold a plenary session and ask the children to share their mnemonics with each other and discuss which ones are the most memorable, unusual or funny.

● **Photocopiable page 73 'Writing rules'**
In this activity, the children look at groups of words to find a common spelling pattern and write a rule for each group. Before beginning the activity, ask the children to say a spelling rule that they can remember and how it helps them with their spelling. Ask them to suggest any exceptions to their rule. When the children have completed the activity, hold a plenary session to share their rules. Were they all similar? Challenge the children to think of any exceptions and ask if there are any sets of words on the photocopiable sheet that have no exceptions to the spelling rule.

Further ideas

● **Word chain:** Hold a plenary activity where the children form a circle and try to create an unbroken chain of words beginning with the last letter of the previous word. Tell the children they should listen carefully to each other to avoid repetition as this could result in a two-word chain (for example, repeating the words *table* and *elephant*).
● **Challenge:** Challenge the children to find a long word with the highest number of short words within it.

What's on the CD-ROM

On the CD-ROM you will find:
● Printable versions of all three photocopiable pages.
● Answers to 'Hard c and soft c'.

Establishing rules

Hard and soft c

■ Find all the words in the ring. Each new word begins with the last letter of the previous one. Write the words in two columns.

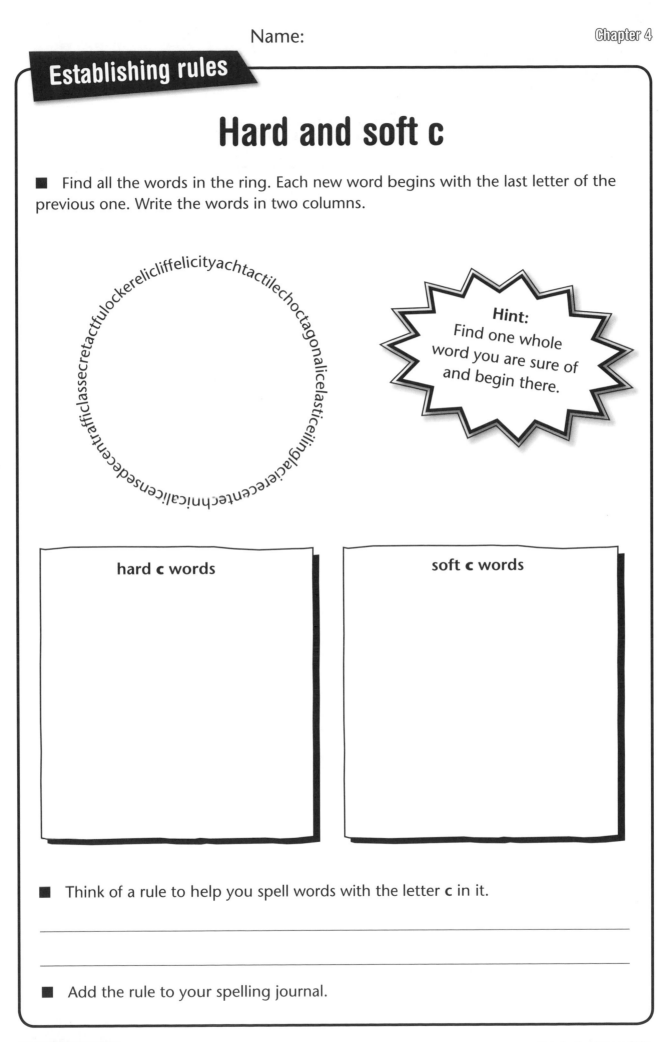

trafficlassecretactfulockerelicliffelicityachtactilechoctagonalicelasticeilinglacierecentechnicalicensedecent

Hint:
Find one whole word you are sure of and begin there.

hard **c** words	soft **c** words

■ Think of a rule to help you spell words with the letter **c** in it.

_____

_____

■ Add the rule to your spelling journal.

Name:

Establishing rules

Mnemonics

■ A mnemonic is a phrase or rhyme that helps you remember how to spell the tricky part of a word. For example, if you remember 'Is a cess pit necessary?' you will always remember to use one **c** and double **s** in the word *necessary*.

■ Find a word within these longer words and write your own mnemonic for each word.

long word	word-within-word
character	
mnemonic:	
descent	
mnemonic:	
signature	
mnemonic:	
soldier	
mnemonic:	
relevant	
mnemonic:	
separate	
mnemonic:	
government	
mnemonic:	
business	
mnemonic:	

■ Add the mnemonics to your spelling journal.

PHOTOCOPIABLE   ■SCHOLASTIC
www.scholastic.co.uk

Establishing rules

Writing rules

■ Look at these groups of words. Write your own rules to help you remember how to spell them.

all	already
skill	skilful
full	fulfil
well	welcome
will	wilful

My rule: _____

bitter	biting
dinner	diner
latter	later
hopper	hoping

My rule: _____

picnic	picnicking
traffic	trafficking
mimic	mimicking
panic	panicking

My rule: _____

happy	happiness
beauty	beautiful
fury	furious
plenty	plentiful

My rule: _____

hope	hoping
wake	waking
ride	riding
write	writing

My rule: _____

■ Add the rules to your spelling journal.

Illustrations © 2009, Rupert Van Wyk/Beehive Illustration.

Assessment

Assessment grid

The following grid shows the main objectives and activities covered in this chapter. You can use the grid to locate activities that cover a particular focus that you are keen to monitor.

Objective	Page	Activity title
To investigate and learn a range of spelling rules and their exceptions.	61 62 63 64	Which /k/ am I? Changing y to i Doubling consonants Which order?
To investigate and learn the spellings of words with unstressed vowels.	66 67 68 69	Hidden vowels -ary, -ory or -ery? Missing vowels Roots
To learn and invent a range of spelling rules.	71 72 73	Hard and soft c Mnemonics Writing rules

Tricky words	I wrote	Tricky part	Correct spelling
queue	que	unusual vowel pattern 'ueue'	queue

Use spelling journals to provide evidence for assessing ongoing work.

Observation and record keeping

This assessment activity requires children to choose three words from their own knowledge that prove a number of common spelling rules. The rules are those that have been covered in the chapter. This gives you the opportunity to observe if the children have fully understood the rules that were covered.

While the children are completing the photocopiable sheets in this chapter, encourage them to keep a spelling journal, for example, recording how well they did and any difficulties they encountered. Encourage them to write down any words that were tricky for them and any mistakes they made. A note of appropriate rules, patterns and mnemonics will also be helpful to them. For example:

Assessment activity

● **What you need**
Photocopiable page 75 'Prove it!' for each child, writing materials.

● **What to do**
Provide each child with a copy of the assessment activity on the photocopiable sheet. Remind the children of the rules they have been inventing during this chapter and the rules they remembered before doing the activity on photocopiable page 73 'Writing rules'. Explain that learning spelling rules is only valuable if they can put them into practice. Ask them to write three words to demonstrate their knowledge of each of the spelling rules on the assessment sheet.

Differentiation

● Go through each rule of the assessment activity orally with less confident learners before they attempt them independently.
● Extend the activity for more confident learners by asking them to write four words or more. You may also wish to ask them to add another rule with examples on the back of the sheet.

Further learning

● **Tenses:** Provide some word cards showing the present tense of a variety of verbs (such as *jump, hop, sleep*). Invite the children to add '-ing' and '-ed' to the verbs to make new words. What patterns did they apply? Investigate if the rules are the same for both suffixes.

Assessment

Prove it!

■   Write down three words that prove each of these rules.

i before **e**

1 _____ 2 _____ 3 _____

i before **e** except after **c**

1 _____ 2 _____ 3 _____

Double the final consonant when adding a suffix that begins with a vowel.

1 _____ 2 _____ 3 _____

Words with **a** long vowel sound and final letter **e** drop the **e** when adding a suffix that begins with a vowel.

1 _____ 2 _____ 3 _____

Words with two or more syllables that end with the sound /ik/ are spelled **ic**.

1 _____ 2 _____ 3 _____

Plurals of words that end in a consonant and **y** drop the **y** and add **ies**.

1 _____ 2 _____ 3 _____

When adding a prefix that ends with **ll**, drop the final **l**.

1 _____ 2 _____ 3 _____

Illustration © 2009, Rupert Van Wyk/Beehive Illustration.

■SCHOLASTIC   **PHOTOCOPIABLE**   www.scholastic.co.uk

Chapter 5

Sounding out and analysing

Introduction

This chapter focuses on using phonemes and syllables to help spell tricky long words, finding known words within words to help remember spellings and revising the spelling of the long vowel phonemes /ai/, /ee/, /igh/, /oa/, /oo/ and /yoo/. These are spelling skills that will help children overcome some of the most commonly misspelled words. Throughout the chapter, children are encouraged to investigate, explore and record their findings in spelling journals. Independent investigations and explorations about the structure of words will allow children to discover patterns and conventions for themselves which can help them to become more confident spellers.

In this chapter

Phonemes and syllables page 78	To use phonemes and syllables to learn the spelling of longer tricky words.
Long vowel sounds page 82	To revise the spelling of long vowel phonemes.
Words within words page 86	To use words within words as an aid to spelling longer words.
Assessment page 90	Activities and ideas to assess knowledge of sounding out and analysing.

Poster notes

Long vowel phonemes (page 77)
Display this poster while the children are completing the three sections of this chapter. Encourage the children to use sticky notes to add words they discover with long vowel sounds from all the activities and from their personal reading. Three different spelling patterns for each phoneme are given as examples from which to start. Review the poster from time to time, discussing the different spelling variations for the same sound.

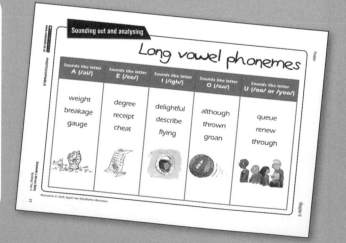

Long vowel phonemes

Sounding out and analysing

Sounds like letter A (/ai/)	Sounds like letter E (/ee/)	Sounds like letter I (/igh/)	Sounds like letter O (/oa/)	Sounds like letter U (/oo/ or /yoo/)
weight	degree	delightful	although	queue
breakage	receipt	describe	thrown	renew
gauge	cheat	flying	groan	through

Illustrations © 2009, Rupert Van Wyk/Beehive Illustration.

Phonemes and syllables

Objective

To use phonemes and syllables to learn the spelling of longer tricky words.

Background knowledge

Learning and using the technique of dividing words into syllables and sounds can help children learn the spellings of tricky words. This is particularly useful when spelling longer words with unstressed letters. Providing the children with plenty of practice in deconstructing and analysing the spelling conventions of these types of words will help them to work out the most plausible spelling when they need to spell complex words in a writing context. The conventional way of dividing words into syllables is to include a vowel sound in each syllable and to split double letters. Breaking a word up into syllables with double letters and unstressed vowels, then pronouncing each syllable separately, will help children remember the correct spelling by giving them a visual and auditory image of the word.

Activities

● **Photocopiable page 79 'Letters and sounds'**
As the children count the number of letters in words and then their phonemes, they reinforce the knowledge that the number of letters does not always equate with the sounds the letters represent. As a follow up to the session, talk about the range of different graphemes that represent the phonemes. Discuss the children's results and iron out any discrepancies.

● **Photocopiable page 80 'Syllables'**
Children are given 20 words to sort into six balloons according to the number of syllables in each word. Long complex words containing double consonants and consonant clusters or blends can pose a problem for some spellers. Learning how to break such words down into syllables can help the children remember where double consonants and blends occur.

● **Photocopiable page 81 'Which word?'**
Children are given clues and the number of syllables and or phonemes to find words and complete a word grid. The answers are provided in a word box. However, in order to challenge more confident learners you can mask the word box before copying the page. For less confident children, write one of the answers in the grid for them so that they can use the letters to help work out the other words.

Further ideas

● **Syllable cards:** Create syllable cards and ask the children to mix and match them to make words. Suggest that they check the words they have made in a dictionary.

● **Add a syllable:** Play a cumulative word game. Begin with a one-syllable word beginning with 'a'. The next child says a two-syllable word, then another adds a three-syllable word and so on until they run out of words and change to the next letter of the alphabet.

● **Wall chart:** Make a wall chart of words with three, four, five and more syllables and encourage the children to add words from their reading. Challenge them to find words with as many syllables as possible!

What's on the CD-ROM

On the CD-ROM you will find:
● Printable versions of all three photocopiable pages.
● Answers to all three photocopiable pages.
● Interactive versions of 'Syllables' and 'Which word?'.

Phonemes and syllables

Letters and sounds

■ How many letters and sounds do these words contain?

■ Count the letters first and then count the phonemes (sounds). Write your answers in the boxes. The first one has been done for you.

Word	Number of letters	Number of phonemes
emphasise	9	7
exaggeration		
miscellaneous		
catastrophe		
conscience		
temperature		
committee		
enough		
architecture		
delicious		
mysterious		
attention		
outrageous		
embarrass		
sequence		
patience		
apostrophe		

■SCHOLASTIC   PHOTOCOPIABLE
www.scholastic.co.uk

Name:

Syllables

■ Count the number of syllables in each word and write the words into the corresponding balloons. Remember, each syllable needs a vowel or **y**. Double letters are split between syllables (for example, at/tack).

difference	embarrass	reference	marvellous
familiarity	vaccination	outrageous	temperature
poisonous	parallel	weight	miscellaneous
jewellery	consequently	imaginary	rehearsal
illiterate	whereas	exaggerated	mnemonic

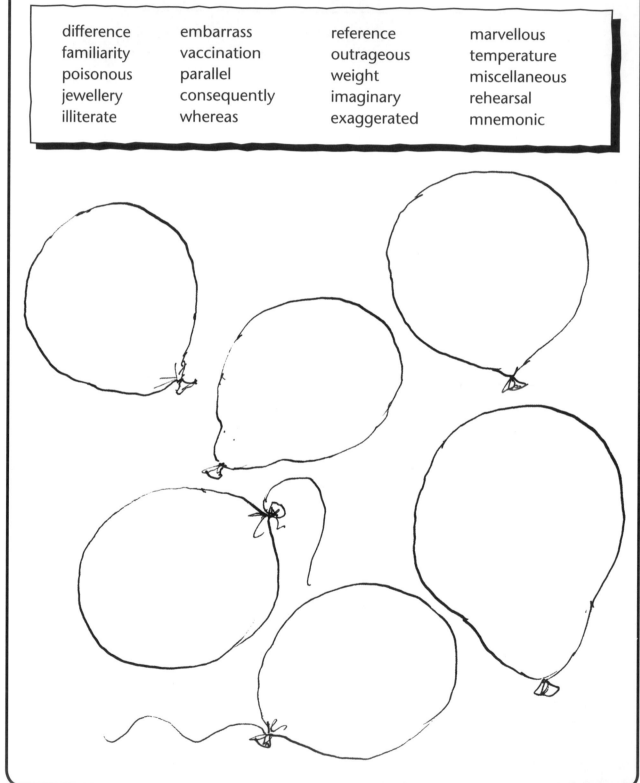

PHOTOCOPIABLE

■SCHOLASTIC
www.scholastic.co.uk

Illustrations © 2009, Rupert Van Wyk/Beehive Illustration.

Phonemes and syllables

Which word?

■   Answer the clues to complete the word grid. Choose the answers from the word box below.

Clues

1. I can *float* in the sky with 5 phonemes and 2 syllables.
2. Showing *possession* or *omission*, I've only got 4 syllables.
3. I *own up* to having 6 phonemes.
4. I am *joined* by only 1 syllable.
5. I *don't get paid* and I have 3 syllables.
6. A *statement* has 10 phonemes but only 4 syllables.
7. A *formation* with 7 sounds and 3 syllables.
8. My *stress* is on the first of 3 syllables.
9. I *dash between words* with 7 phonemes.

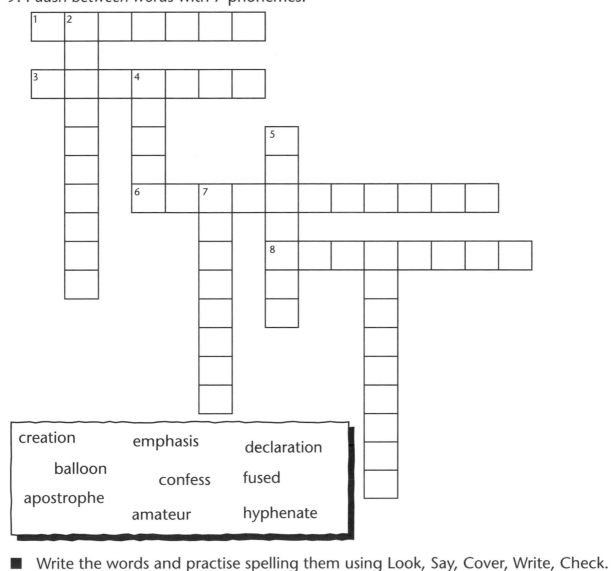

creation   emphasis   declaration

balloon   confess   fused

apostrophe

amateur   hyphenate

■   Write the words and practise spelling them using Look, Say, Cover, Write, Check.

Long vowel sounds

Objective

To revise the spelling of long vowel phonemes.

Background knowledge

One of the problems children face in spelling is deciding which way to spell a word with a long vowel sound. There are many ways to spell long vowel sounds in English and only a few rules to follow. Remind the children that long vowel sounds usually use two or more vowels. These can be next to each other (as in *foal*) or separated by a single consonant (as in *fade*). Exposure to the words, combined with inventing mnemonics, can help the children to remember which variation to use.

Activities

● **Photocopiable page 83 'Sort the vowels'**
The children group words according to their vowel sound from a selection of words with long vowel sounds. Before they begin, remind them of the long vowel sounds: /ai/ (sounds like the name of the letter 'a'), /ee/ (sounds like the name of the letter 'e'), /igh/ (sounds like the name of the letter 'i'), /oa/ (sounds like the name of the letter 'o'), and /yoo/ (sounds like the name of the letter 'u'). As they write the words into the correct balloon they are exposed to several ways of spelling each of the phonemes. They then group them by spelling pattern and identify which they find tricky to spell. Follow up the work by asking the children to group the words to organise them by spelling pattern. Ask them which words they find tricky to remember. Suggest that they invent a mnemonic for each tricky word – for example, *Sleigh: Snow Leaves Everyone In Good Humour*.

● **Photocopiable page 84 'Short or long?'**
The children are asked to sort a selection of words with 'oe' and 'ei' spelling patterns into short or long vowel sounds and then regroup them by the sound the vowel makes in the words. The 'ei' spelling pattern can be tricky for children in words such as *leisure* and *heifer* when it has a short vowel sound. Support children who need extra help by reading the list of words aloud together before they attempt the activity. Challenge more confident learners to add other words that have different /oe/ and /ei/ vowel sounds to the list.

● **Photocopiable page 85 'Words and ways'**
Children are challenged to write as many words with different ways of writing the long vowel sound /ai/. Support children who need extra help by brainstorming as many words as they can think of orally before beginning the activity. Suggest that the children also refer to their personal dictionaries or word banks for ideas. Challenge more confident learners further by giving them a time limit.

Further ideas

● **Vowel fans:** Read the words from the first two photocopiable sheets aloud to the children and ask them to use vowel fans to show the spelling patterns of the long vowel sounds.

● **Unusual words:** Create a wall display of unusual words that the children find when reading. Encourage them to decorate the letters that make the vowel sound.

 **What's on the CD-ROM**

On the CD-ROM you will find:
● Printable versions of all three photocopiable pages.
● Answers to 'Sort the vowels' and 'Short or long?'.
● Interactive versions of 'Sort the vowels' and 'Short or long?'.

Long vowel sounds

Sort the vowels

■ Listen to the long vowel sounds in these words. Decide which letter name the vowel sounds like. Sort the words into the matching balloons.

cute	stone
cold	quay
fly	shoulder
pail	freedom
apply	use
flight	toad
sleigh	queue
cue	date
tight	anew
these	straight
white	grown
delight	receive
height	main
stray	neigh
relieve	wallow
oboe	weight
few	moan
seat	machine
people	kite

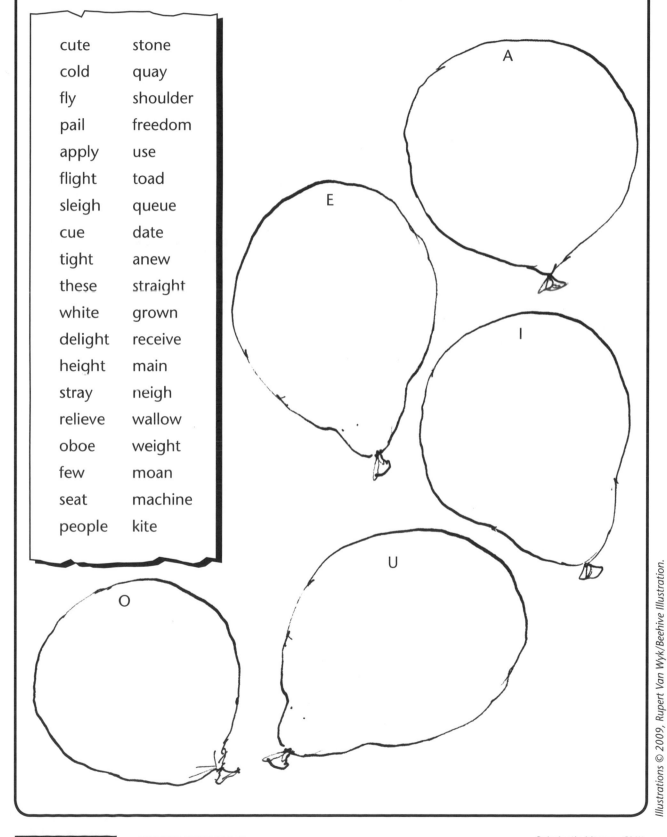

Illustrations © 2009, Rupert Van Wyk/Beehive Illustration.

Name:

Long vowel sounds

Short or long?

■ These words all use the **oe** or the **ei** spelling pattern. Say each word aloud and decide if the letters make a long or a short vowel sound. Write them into the correct column.

heifer	doe	eiderdown	caffeine
canoe	rein	seize	foetal
heir	height	amoeba	forfeit
leisure	sloe	their	poem
shoe	foreign	onomatopoeia	ceiling
feign	woe	veil	abseil

Short vowel sound	Long vowel sound

■ On a piece of paper, group the words according to the sound the letters **oe** and **ei** make.

PHOTOCOPIABLE

Long vowel sounds

Words and ways

■ How many different words can you find that have a long **a** vowel sound?
(/**ai**/ – sounds like the letter name **a**.) Write them into the correct column.

ay as in *play*	a–e as in *plate*	ei as in *freight*	ai as in *train*	ea as in *great*	ey as in *they*

■ Which ones do you find tricky? Write them in your spelling journal and practise
them using Look, Say, Cover, Write, Check.

Words within words

● Photocopiable page 88 'Now I remember!'

Objective

To use words within words as an aid to spelling longer words.

Background knowledge

Hunting for shorter words within longer words means that children are required to read the sound of each letter in the word and then combine it with the subsequent letter, slowly building up the letter combinations with the following letters to make other words. Thus, in *threaten* they work through the word to find the first obvious word (*threat*), then *ate* and finally *ten*. This investigative approach appeals particularly to visual learning styles. Working with a partner to find words within words will help children whose preferred learning style is auditory by sounding the letters and reading the new words aloud together. It may also help the children to remember the tricky parts of words by giving them an image of part of the word in their mind. If children can use the spelling of known words that occur in longer words it can help them spell longer words correctly.

Activities

● **Photocopiable page 87 'Wordsearch'**
The children are challenged to find ten given long words in a wordsearch grid and then to find and write down any shorter words within the long words. Support children who need extra help by reading the list of words before beginning the activity. If children need further support, write *leisurely* on the board as a demonstration. Work through the word by writing *leisure, is, sure, surely,* and *rely* to illustrate how to use each letter as an investigation point.

● **Photocopiable page 88 'Now I remember!'**
As the children find a shorter word within ten longer words, they write their own memory-jogger or mnemonic using the short word to help them spell the longer word. Before beginning the activity, look together through the words on the photocopiable sheet and ask the children to suggest which parts of the words are the tricky bits that they could get wrong. Explain that if they can find a word in the tricky bit for their mnemonic it will help them remember it. For example, a mnemonic that uses *out* will not be particularly helpful when spelling *outrageous* but *rage* would be very helpful.

● **Photocopiable page 89 'Pelmanism'**
In this activity the children are given word cards of 10 long words and a further 20 short words. Two short words are taken from within each of the long words. The children play a form of Pelmanism to identify the matching pairs of short and long words. This can be played in pairs or individually. Ask the children to pick and read one long word card, then turn over a short word card. If they match, they can be removed from the set. Set a further challenge to find the long word and both short words to clear all the cards. In a plenary session after completing the game, hold up each long word card and ask the children if they can find any other words within each word.

Further ideas

● **Finding short words:** Challenge the children over a period of time to find a word that has the highest number of shorter words within it. For example, the word *inoperable* has six short words within it. Can they find another word with more than six?
● **New words:** Provide the children with a short word, such as *ten*). Ask them to find as many new words that have the short word within it (for example, *tension, attention, potential* and so on).
● **Wall display:** Make a decorated wall display of long words with words within words coloured and written in different styles.

What's on the CD-ROM

On the CD-ROM you will find:
● Printable versions of all three photocopiable pages.
● Answers to 'Wordsearch'.

Words within words

Wordsearch

■ Find the words below in the wordsearch grid. They all have a shorter word or words within them. Highlight the long words in the wordsearch and write the shorter words at the foot of the page.

| commencement | malevolent | crumbled | enlargement | threatening |
| cooperate | leisurely | embarrass | treated | strainer |

c	o	m	m	e	n	c	e	m	e	n	t	f
o	q	a	w	e	c	r	v	b	n	a	e	k
o	u	l	e	i	s	u	r	e	l	y	n	s
p	d	e	v	m	i	m	o	g	a	m	d	e
e	j	v	c	e	m	b	a	r	r	a	s	s
r	i	o	a	b	s	l	a	w	g	u	t	h
a	h	l	e	l	a	e	n	s	e	t	r	i
t	r	e	a	t	e	d	y	u	m	p	a	u
e	y	n	u	p	s	j	f	a	e	w	i	t
t	a	t	h	r	e	a	t	e	n	i	n	g
s	r	y	g	u	r	p	l	z	t	a	e	y
w	u	c	k	y	d	o	o	m	s	t	r	y

Short words

Name:

Words within words

Now I remember!

■ Find a word within each of these words and use it to write a memory-jogger or mnemonic to help you spell it. The first one has been done for you.

argument   short word _____gum_____

Don't ever have an argument about gum _____

outrageous   short word _____

_____

participate   short word _____

_____

desperately   short word _____

_____

piece   short word _____

_____

comfortable   short word _____

_____

practical   short word _____

_____

accountant   short word _____

_____

secretary   short word _____

_____

appearance   short word _____

_____

explanation   short word _____

_____

PHOTOCOPIABLE   ■SCHOLASTIC
www.scholastic.co.uk

Words within words

Pelmanism

■ Cut out the word cards and place them face down on a table. Pick up two cards and when you find a long word and a short word that is also in the long word, put them to one side. When you have matched ten long words with ten shorter ones the game is finished.

chocolate	late	cola
business	sin	bus
definite	fin	nit
fortunately	tuna	ate
proportion	prop	port
potential	pot	ten
peaceful	pea	ace
outrageous	rag	out
vegetable	get	able
government	go	men

■ SCHOLASTIC
www.scholastic.co.uk   **PHOTOCOPIABLE**

Assessment

Assessment grid

The following grid shows the main objectives and activities covered in this chapter. You can use the grid to locate activities that cover a particular focus that you are keen to monitor.

Objective	Page	Activity title
To use phonemes and syllables to learn the spelling of longer tricky words.	79 80 81	Letters and sounds Syllables Which word?
To revise the spelling of long vowel phonemes.	83 84 85	Sort the vowels Short or long? Words and ways
To use words within words as an aid to spelling longer words.	87 88 89	Wordsearch Now I remember! Pelmanism

Observation and record keeping

This assessment activity requires children to practise all the work covered in the chapter. Some of the words in the activity have not been used before but others will be familiar. This gives you the opportunity to observe whether the children have a firm grasp of the strategies covered.

While the children are completing the photocopiable sheets in this chapter, encourage them to keep a spelling journal, for example, recording how well they did and any difficulties they encountered. Encourage them to write down any words that were tricky for them and any mistakes they made. A note of appropriate rules, patterns and mnemonics will also be helpful to them. For example:

Tricky words	I wrote	Tricky part	Correct spelling
separate	seperate	par	separate

Use spelling journals to provide evidence for assessing ongoing work.

Assessment activity

● **What you need**
Photocopiable page 91 'Analysing words' for each child, writing materials.
● **What to do**
Provide each child with a copy of the photocopiable sheet. Explain that during this activity they will be demonstrating their understanding of the work practised in the course of this chapter – counting phonemes and syllables, finding a word within other words and identifying the long vowel sounds. Check that the children understand that there are four parts to the activity: before they begin, ask them to say what a phoneme is, how to divide a word into syllables and how they should begin looking for words within words.

Differentiation

● Go through each word of the assessment activity orally with less confident children before they attempt them independently. You may also reduce the number of tasks by, for example, asking them to only count the syllables and find the 'words within words'.
● Extend more confident children by asking them to complete the task in a limited time.

Further learning

● **Syllable split:** Write a word on the board and ask the children to count the phonemes or syllables within a limited time. You could use the number of phonemes as the number of seconds allowed for the challenge.
● **Running together:** Encourage the children to think carefully about breaking words into syllables and running them together again to say the complete word.
● **Letters and phonemes:** Challenge the children to find words that have the same number of letters and phonemes, beginning with three-letter words and gradually increasing in length.

Assessment

Analysing words

■ Count the phonemes and syllables. Now underline a word within each word. Draw a circle around the long vowel sounds.

Phonemes		Syllables
	encyclopedia	
	miscellaneous	
	committee	
	neighbour	
	material	
	emphasise	
	phoenix	
	earthquake	
	frightened	
	weight	
	previous	
	microscope	

Chapter 6
Applying and using knowledge

Introduction

In this chapter the activities enable the children to revise and revisit important spelling rules and conventions and give them the opportunity to apply their knowledge about previous spelling. In particular, the ideas in this chapter focus on letter strings and spelling patterns that the children often find tricky or confusing, such as the spelling of words ending '-ant' and '-ance', '-ent' and '-ence'; the different ways of pronouncing words with the letter string 'our'; and words ending in '-ure'. In addition, 'ie' and 'ei' words are explored along with silent letters, contractions and spelling strategies that use rhyme, analogy and probability.

In this chapter

Letter strings page 94	To revise the spelling of words with letter strings '-ant', '-ance', '-ent', '-ence', 'our' and '-ure'.
Tricky spellings page 98	To secure the spelling of words with silent letters, 'ie' and 'ei' spelling patterns and contracted verbs.
Making analogies page 102	To practise spelling using analogies with known words. To use visual and aural strategies to aid spelling.
Assessment page 106	Activities and ideas to assess applying and using knowledge.

Poster notes

Look, Say, Cover, Write, Check (page 93)
This poster can be used and displayed whenever children are using the strategy of Look, Say, Cover, Write, Check to practise their spelling. It extends the approach by adding tips for each section and encourages children to use their sense of hearing and sound. This multi-sensory approach to learning the spellings of a group of words is a trusted and effective technique that can be used by all abilities. Once children are familiar with it, they can apply it to any words they find difficult.

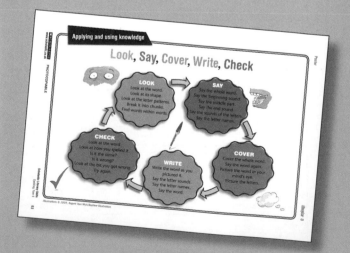

Applying and using knowledge

Look, Say, Cover, Write, Check

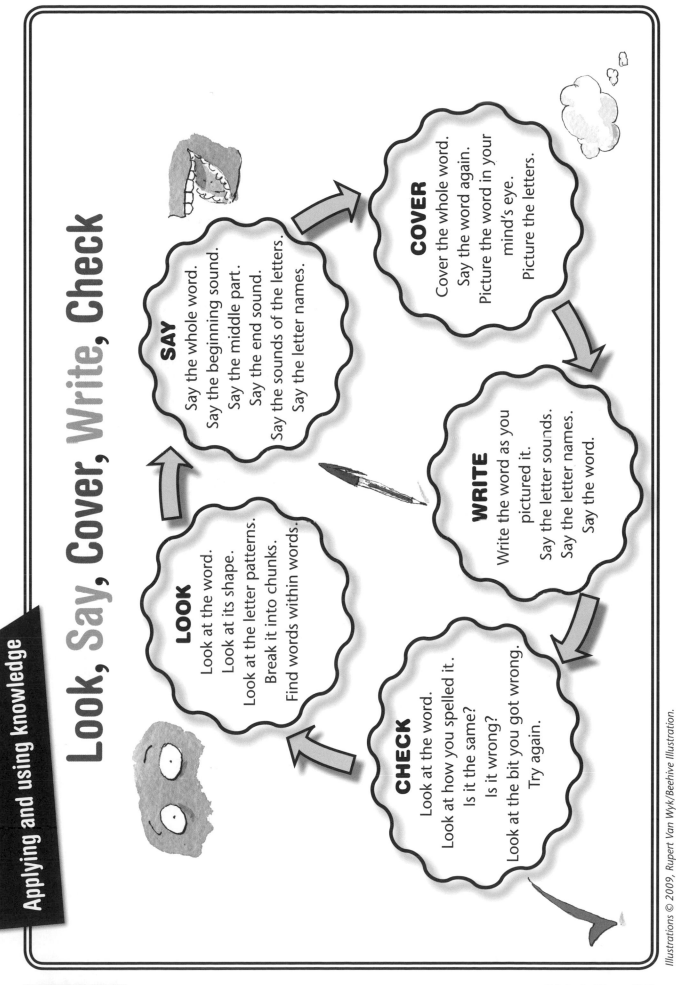

SAY

Say the whole word.
Say the beginning sound.
Say the middle part.
Say the end sound.
Say the sounds of the letters.
Say the letter names.

COVER

Cover the whole word.
Say the word again.
Picture the word in your mind's eye.
Picture the letters.

LOOK

Look at the word.
Look at its shape.
Look at the letter patterns.
Break it into chunks.
Find words within words.

WRITE

Write the word as you pictured it.
Say the letter sounds.
Say the letter names.
Say the word.

CHECK

Look at the word.
Look at how you spelled it.
Is it the same?
Is it wrong?
Look at the bit you got wrong.
Try again.

Illustrations © 2009, Rupert Van Wyk/Beehive Illustration.

Letter strings

To revise the spelling of words with letter strings '-ant', '-ance', '-ent', '-ence', 'our' and '-ure'.

Background knowledge

By investigating words ending with '-ant' and '-ance', '-ent' and '-ence', children become aware of the relationship between the pairs of words and the spelling pattern. This can help children who might easily spell *abundant* but struggle with *abundance*. The letter strings 'our' and '-ure' can often confuse children. Children can be helped to spell the words by appreciating where the different patterns commonly occur in words: 'our' can come in the beginning, middle or end of a word and have different pronunciations; '-ure' can be a suffix added to a root word to make a noun, or may be an integral part of a word such as *future*.

Activities

● **Photocopiable page 95 'Relationships'**
In this activity the children do three short activities to explore the relationship between words that change from '-ant' to '-ance' and from '-ent' to '-ence' and vice versa. As they work through the activities, encourage them to say the sentences aloud and over-pronounce the 'e' or 'a' sounds. After completing the activities, encourage them to invent mnemonics to remind them whether the word uses '-ant', '-ance', '-ent' or '-ence' (for example: *I see a distant ant*).

● **Photocopiable page 96 'Finding our'**
The letter string 'our' is pronounced in different ways in different words and can occur at the beginning, middle or end of words. As the children find the 'our' words in the grid, encourage them to say the words aloud so that they are exposed to the different ways of pronouncing the 'our' letter string. As they come across words in their reading, encourage them to add other examples with the same pronunciation to their spelling journals.

● **Photocopiable page 97 'Are you sure?'**
In this activity the children complete three short sections focusing on roots and suffixes and complete words with the '-ure' letter string. Understanding the meaning of words is essential to the correct use and spelling of words – therefore, as well as applying knowledge of roots and suffixes, the activity includes making a correct choice of vocabulary to complete sentences in a cloze procedure.

Further ideas

● **Word a day:** Challenge the children to use a word a day from each of the activities in their own writing.
● **Spelling journals:** As the children encounter other words with the same letter strings in their personal reading, encourage them to add them to their spelling journals.
● **Our clues:** Working in pairs, provide the children with five or six words taken from each of the photocopiable sheets and ask them to think of a clue that will help their partner guess the word. The partner then writes the answer and takes a turn to think of a clue for a different word.

What's on the CD-ROM

On the CD-ROM you will find:
● Printable versions of all three photocopiable pages.
● Answers to all three photocopiable pages.
● Interactive versions of 'Relationships' and 'Are you sure?'.

Letter strings

Relationships

■ Write the adjective or the noun that is missing from these sentences. The first one has been done as an example.

1. In the distance I could see a **distant** tower.

2. He proved his innocence and walked away as an _____ man.

3. The intelligent boy worked hard to show his _____.

4. An elegant woman walks with grace and _____.

5. The disobedient dog was taken to _____ classes.

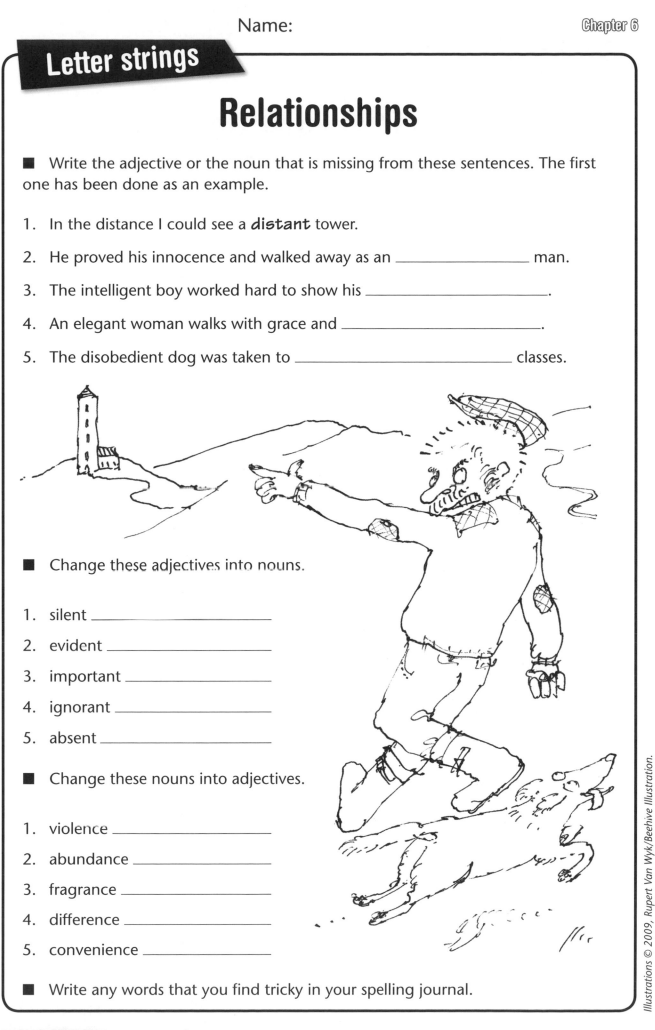

■ Change these adjectives into nouns.

1. silent _____

2. evident _____

3. important _____

4. ignorant _____

5. absent _____

■ Change these nouns into adjectives.

1. violence _____

2. abundance _____

3. fragrance _____

4. difference _____

5. convenience _____

■ Write any words that you find tricky in your spelling journal.

Illustrations © 2009, Rupert Van Wyk/Beehive Illustration.

Name:

Letter strings

Finding our

■ Hidden in the wordsearch grid are eight words with the letter string **our** in them. Find the words and then say them aloud. Write the words in a list and practise spelling them using Look, Say, Cover, Write, Check.

q	u	w	t	e	t	u	i	p	a
s	d	h	j	d	f	c	b	a	k
t	r	j	o	r	e	a	j	n	c
p	s	v	u	y	g	u	n	z	e
c	o	u	r	t	e	s	y	i	o
o	u	l	i	a	e	o	g	s	v
n	o	c	s	s	p	u	r	i	o
t	w	a	h	o	u	r	l	y	e
o	i	e	o	h	w	o	b	u	p
u	t	p	s	c	s	l	d	w	u
r	e	f	l	o	u	r	t	i	o
y	r	o	x	u	r	t	e	h	a
s	u	u	w	r	u	m	o	u	r
o	t	r	r	i	p	y	u	o	n
d	y	u	i	e	e	a	j	b	f
a	g	m	t	r	f	k	s	s	l

■ Group the words in your spelling journal based on the sound that the letter string makes (such as *hour* and *flour*; *pour* and *your*). Add other words to the groups as you come across them in your reading.

PHOTOCOPIABLE ■SCHOLASTIC
www.scholastic.co.uk

Letter strings

Are you sure?

■ Match the root word to the **-ure** words by drawing a line.

moist
depart
please
fail
architect

departure
architecture
moisture
pleasure
failure

■ Choose the correct **-ure** word to fit the space in these sentences.

exposure	treasure	adventure	future

1. Our trip to see the whales was quite an _____.

2. The map showing the buried _____ was very old and crumpled.

3. "I wonder what the _____ will bring," mused the fortune teller.

4. Too much _____ to the sun isn't good for your skin.

■ Which of these words adds a suffix to a verb to make a noun? _____

■ Write the root word for each of these **-ure** words.

1. mixture _____

2. composure _____

3. creature _____

4. pressure _____

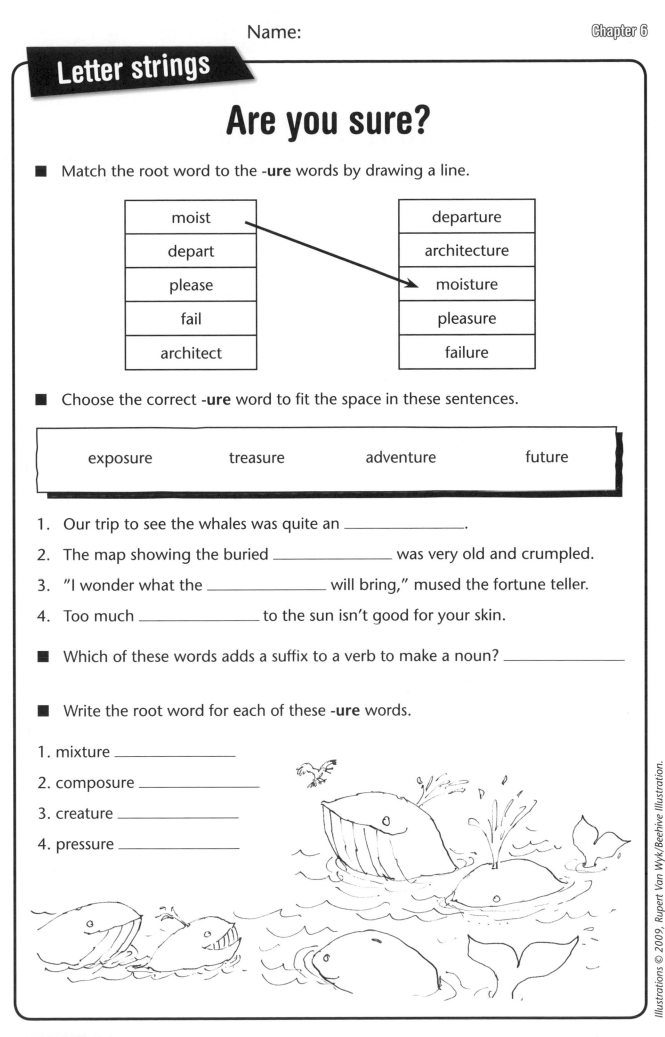

Illustrations © 2009, Rupert Van Wyk/Beehive Illustration.

Tricky spellings

Objective

To secure the spelling of words with silent letters, 'ie' and 'ei' spelling patterns and contracted verbs.

Background knowledge

The 'i before e' rule is well known, but the spelling convention relies on the sound produced by the digraph. For words that contain a long /ee/ sound, 'ie' is the convention but not when it comes after 'c' (for example, *receive*). Words containing a long /ai/ sound use 'ei' (such as *freight*). Other 'ei' words can have various vowel sounds, such as *foreign, weird, height*.

Silent letters in words can also be tricky. Children need to learn these words and it can help them if they say each sound when practising their spelling. Stressing the silent letter can help them remember – for example, pronouncing the 'k' when saying *knock*, or the 'b' in *comb*. Simple errors with apostrophes of contraction can lower a child's spelling level. They need to be taught that the apostrophe is placed where a letter is omitted.

Activities

● **Photocopiable page 99 'ie and ei sounds'**
As the children group words with the 'ie'/'ei' digraph they should understand how the pronunciation of the word affects the spelling convention. For example, that the rule *'i' before 'e' except after 'c'* only applies when the word rhymes with *bee*; that words that rhyme with *play* are spelled 'ei'.

● **Photocopiable page 100 'Silent letters'**
Before beginning the activity, ask the children to brainstorm words they know that contain silent letters. In the activity, children answer clues to spell words with silent letters and practise their spelling using Look, Say, Cover, Write, Check. Encourage the children to say each answer aloud and pronounce the silent letter as they speak the word.

● **Photocopiable page 101 'Apostrophes'**
In this activity the children revise and secure their use of apostrophes while rewriting sentences using contracted verb forms. Support less confident children by reading each sentence aloud first and re-reading with contracted verbs. Then discuss which letters have been omitted.

Further ideas

● **Sounds like:** Make a class display of 'ei' and 'ie' words grouped according to their sound. Encourage the children to add to the display when they meet more words in their personal reading.
● **Silent letters:** List silent letters as column headings on a large piece of paper that is displayed prominently (for example 'p', 'b', 'w', 'h', 'k') and add words that use each letter.

What's on the CD-ROM

On the CD-ROM you will find:
● Printable versions of all three photocopiable pages.
● Answers to all three photocopiable pages.
● Interactive versions of 'ie and ei sounds' and 'Silent letters'.

Tricky spellings

ie and ei sounds

■ Group these words by the sound **ie** and **ei** make.

shield	pie
eight	freight
beige	leisure
believe	their
hygiene	weigh
rein	height
field	heir
shriek	pierce
foreign	sleigh
receive	fierce
friend	view
deceit	perceive
either	sleight

sounds like *few*

sounds like *way*

sounds like *by*

sounds like *ear*

sounds like *bend*

sounds like *bee*

sounds like *fair*

■ Which words are exceptions to the following rule: '**i** before **e** except after **c** when it rhymes with *bee*'?

Name:

Tricky spellings

Silent letters

■ The answers to these clues are all words with silent letters. Write the answers and circle the silent letter, then practise spelling them using Look, Say, Cover, Write, Check. As you practise, say each letter sound aloud.

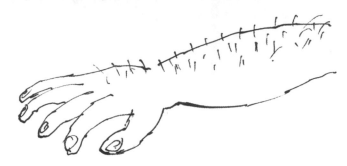

Clue	Answer
This person keeps people or places safe.	g __ __ __ d
You can cut paper with these.	s __ __ __ __ __ s
Joint between your hand and arm.	__ r __ __ t
A serious illness.	__ n __ __ o __ __ a
To make this noise, purse your lips and blow.	w __ __ __ __ __ e
You can cut food with this.	__ __ __ f __
You need these to move your bones.	m __ __ __ __ __ s
Something to make your hair tidy.	c __ __ __
Give up a job.	r __ __ __ __ n
Do this with your ears.	l __ __ __ __ __
Something sung in a church.	h __ __ __
Joints in the fingers.	__ n __ __ __ __ __

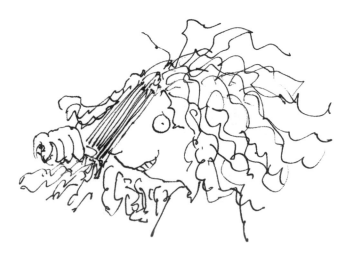

PHOTOCOPIABLE

■SCHOLASTIC
www.scholastic.co.uk

Illustrations © 2009, Rupert Van Wyk/Beehive Illustration.

Tricky spellings

Apostrophes

■ Rewrite these sentences, using an apostrophe to create contracted verb forms (for example, **I am** becomes **I'm**).

1. I cannot find the football. Who will help me look for it?

_____

2. It is under the bed. You have not looked there.

_____

3. It was not there yesterday. I did not think of looking there.

_____

4. They were not going to play hockey. They are going to play football.

_____

5. Who is going to watch the team play? We are all going by bus.

_____

6. We would not like to miss this match. I am sure it will be an exciting one.

_____

7. We have got plenty of time to get there. I will meet you after the game.

_____

8. If we do not hurry, we will not get there on time.

_____

9. Where is the match being played? Is it not at the school?

_____

10. What is the final score? Was it not the best game ever?

_____

■ Write your own rule for using an apostrophe of contraction.

_____

_____

Making analogies

Objectives

To practise spelling using analogies with known words. To use visual and aural strategies to aid spelling.

Background knowledge

In this section the children will be helped to spell tricky or frequently misspelled words by encouraging them first to analyse what is tricky about the word, and then to think about other words that either rhyme or have a related root word. It will also help if they can think of other words with related meanings or the same sort of letter patterns. Encouraging the children to get a picture of the word in their mind's eye will help them to try out different spellings to see which one looks right.

Activities

● **Photocopiable page 103 'What are they?'**
As the children use a root word (verb) to find the related noun, they discover which suffixes are used to describe an occupation. The most commonly used suffixes are '-cian' as in *musician*, '-er' as in *learner* and '-or' as in *doctor*. Other suffixes are '-ist' as in *novelist*, '-ive' as in *detective* and '-on' as in *surgeon*. Support children who may need help by asking them to name some occupations they are familiar with before beginning the activity.

● **Photocopiable page 104 'Related words'**
In this activity the children use clues based on rhyme or analogy to fill in the crossword grid. Support less confident children by filling in one or two of the words before copying the page so that they have other letters as clues to begin with. Challenge more confident spellers by filling in the word *chart* (answer to 2 down) as a starting point for them, but mask the numbers before they begin.

● **Photocopiable page 105 'Sight and sound'**
In this activity the children are given a list of frequently misspelled words and tips to help them analyse each word, thus improving their ability to use the Look, Say, Cover, Write, Check approach effectively. When the children have completed the activity, hold a plenary session to discuss which words they found tricky and why. What were the most frequent mistakes? Ask them to give their opinion about using the Look, Say, Cover, Write, Check strategy – for example, what sort of words does it help them learn?

Further ideas

● **Occupations:** Ask the children to help you to draw up a list of occupations that do not use a suffix, such as *pilot, magistrate, judge*.
● **Spelling journals:** Ask the children to swap spelling journals with a partner. Invite each child to find six words in their partner's journal that were written as tricky words for their partner to learn using Look, Say, Cover, Write, Check. Suggest that they test each other on the words.

What's on the CD-ROM

On the CD-ROM you will find:
● Printable versions of all three photocopiable pages.
● Answers to 'What are they?' and 'Related words'.
● Interactive versions of 'What are they?' and 'Related words'.

Making analogies

What are they?

■ Read each sentence and look at the bold word. Think of the suffix that describes the occupation, and write the answer in the space provided.

1. A person who uses a sewing **machine** is a _____ .

2. A person who works in **politics** is a _____ .

3. A person who **sings** is a _____ .

4. A person who performs **magic** tricks is a _____ .

5. A person who works in **hygiene** is a _____ .

6. A person who writes **novels** is a _____ .

7. A person who **drives** is a _____ .

8. A person who **inspects** things is an _____ .

9. A person who performs **surgery** is a _____ .

10. A person who **detects** crime is a _____ .

11. A person who **dances** is a _____ .

12. A person who plays on a **skateboard** is a _____ .

Illustrations © 2009, Rupert Van Wyk/Beehive Illustration.

Name:

Making analogies

Related words

■ Use the clues to write the related word in the word grid.

CLUES

1. An adjective related to the noun *medicine*.

2. A map or table that rhymes with *part*.

3. An adjective to describe the order of the alphabet.

4. A stretchy material that rhymes with *drastic*.

5. A noun related to the adjective *strong*.

6. A job you have to do that rhymes with *bore*.

7. An adjective related to the noun *fact*.

8. An adjective related to the noun *energy*.

9. Someone who listens is this.

Illustrations © 2009, Rupert Van Wyk/Beehive Illustration.

PHOTOCOPIABLE

SCHOLASTIC
www.scholastic.co.uk

Making analogies

Sight and sound

■ These words can be tricky to spell.

accommodation

symmetrical

embarrassment

audience

potential

burial

conscience

thesaurus

courtesy

ocean

rehearsal

committee

synonym

temperature

successful

possession

column

interrupt

government

evidence

Look!

Look at the shape of these words one at a time.
Make a picture of the word in your mind's eye.
Look at the letters that make each of the sounds.
Chunk the word into syllables.
Find any words within words.

Say!

Say the whole word aloud.
Say each syllable aloud.
Say each sound in the word aloud.
Say each sound, including silent letters, aloud.
Say each letter name aloud.
Say the word again.

■ Now practise spelling the words in the list using Look, Say, Cover, Write, Check.
■ Did you get any wrong?
■ Rewrite them and underline the part where you made a mistake, then follow the Look and Say steps again.

Assessment

Assessment grid

The following grid shows the main objectives and activities covered in this chapter. You can use the grid to locate activities that cover a particular focus that you are keen to monitor.

Objective	Page	Activity title
To revise the spelling of words with letter strings '-ant', '-ance', '-ent', '-ence', 'our' and '-ure'.	95 96 97	Relationships Finding our Are you sure?
To secure the spelling of words with silent letters, 'ie' and 'ei' spelling patterns and contracted verbs.	99 100 101	ie and ei sounds Silent letters Apostrophes
To practise spelling using analogies with known words. To use visual and aural strategies to aid spelling.	103 104 105	What are they? Related words Sight and sound

Observation and record keeping

This assessment activity uses many of the spellings covered in the chapter in a cloze passage. This gives you the opportunity to observe the children's spelling combined with their level of understanding.

While the children are completing the photocopiable sheets in this chapter, encourage them to keep a spelling journal, for example, recording how well they did and any difficulties they encountered. Encourage them to write down any words that were tricky for them and any mistakes they made. A note of appropriate rules, patterns and mnemonics will also be helpful to them. For example:

Tricky words	I wrote	Root	Correct spelling
fragrance	fragrence	fragrant	fragrance

Use spelling journals to provide evidence for assessing ongoing work.

Assessment activity

● **What you need**
Photocopiable page 107 'Fill in the gaps' for each child, writing materials.
● **What to do**
Give the children a photocopiable sheet each. Read the passage aloud to the children with the missing words included. Re-read the passage, asking the children to fill in the spaces on their copies of the photocopiable sheet as you read.

Differentiation

● Read the passage aloud to less confident learners without using the missing words. Discuss word choices with them. Allow them to fill in words that make sense of the passage, but are not necessarily those on the list.
● Extend groups of more confident learners by asking them to complete the cloze passage without reading the missing words to them.

Further learning

● **Human verb phrase:** Using letter cards, have groups of children make a 'human' verb phrase at the front of the class. Give a child an apostrophe card and challenge him/her to replace the letters to make the contracted form of the verb phrase.
● **Silent letters:** When learning words with silent letters, encourage the children to over-pronounce the silent letter as they say the word (for example, *government*).
● **Job titles:** Make a class collection of job titles and encourage the children to find the most unusual ones they can, especially those with a suffix that has not been used in this chapter (such as *puppeteer*).

Assessment

Fill in the gaps

■ Read the passage below to get a sense of what it is about, then fill in the spaces with the missing words. (The missing words are provided in the box at the foot of the page.)

"_____ be nervous. Just do your best, dear," Leila's mother

_____ just before she went onto the stage.

The _____ was broken when Leila picked up her

_____ and gently began to play. She had always wanted

to be a _____ and this was her big chance. Despite the

_____ , she understood the _____ of this

moment and didn't play a single _____ note. Everyone

seemed to be _____ intently and when she finished with a

_____ , the _____ burst into applause.

After the concert her teacher said, "You showed great

_____ of character and _____ on the stage,

Leila. _____ proud of you. I _____ you have an

exciting _____ ahead of you."

"All those extra _____ were worth it," said Leila happily.

believe	musician	silence
importance	wrong	whispered
don't	I'm	composure
rehearsals	listening	strength
guitar	flourish	pressure
audience	future	

■SCHOLASTIC   PHOTOCOPIABLE
www.scholastic.co.uk

Chapter 7

Building on knowledge

Introduction

This chapter focuses on revising and developing children's strategies for remembering spelling conventions and patterns. It includes the conventions for adding prefixes and suffixes, using dictionaries and spelling journals and inventing their own memory-jogging devices. It also includes learning words with unstressed consonants. These are all spelling strategies that the children have been exposed to and practised during the work covered in the earlier chapters of this book. It gives them the opportunity to confirm their understanding. Should any children struggle with any parts of this chapter, you can encourage them to revisit the earlier chapters where the strategy was covered.

In this chapter

Poster notes

Acrostics (page 109)

When children consistently misspell certain words, creating their own acrostic can help to fix the spelling in their minds. The acrostics shown on this poster have been designed to reflect the meanings of some tricky words.

The poster can be displayed as a stimulus for ideas when the children are inventing their own acrostics. Although it is important to encourage the children to think carefully about the meaning of the word when they are writing an acrostic for it, it is more important that they use words that they understand if they are to remember it.

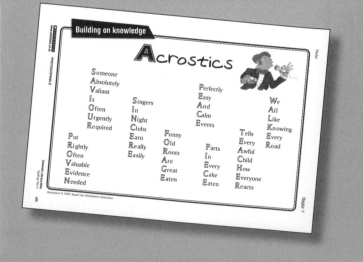

Building on knowledge

Acrostics

Someone
Absolutely
Valiant
Is
Often
Urgently
Required

Put
Rightly
Often
Valuable
Evidence
Needed

Singers
In
Night
Clubs
Earn
Really
Easily

Perfectly
Easy
And
Calm
Events

Funny
Old
Roots
Are
Great
Eaten

Parts
In
Every
Cake
Eaten

We
All
Like
Knowing
Every
Road

Tells
Every
Awful
Child
How
Everyone
Reacts

Illustrations © 2009, Rupert Van Wyk/Beehive Illustration.

Confusables

Objective

To secure the spelling and meaning of easily confused words.

Background knowledge

There are many words in English that are homophones or have very similar sounds but different spellings and can be easily confused. It can help children differentiate between confusing pairs of words when they investigate their meaning and use and work out their own memory tricks for using them accurately. Looking for words within words can help, as can identifying the tricky parts of one of the words and making up a rhyme, acrostic or other mnemonic about the tricky bit. For example, the spellings of the words *principle* and *principal* are often confused. A mnemonic to help differentiate between the words might be: *The principal is my pal!*

Activities

● **Photocopiable page 111 'What's my definition?'**
In this activity the children use a dictionary to find the definitions of pairs of easily confused words and write a sentence for each word to demonstrate the correct usage. An understanding of each word's meaning will help children differentiate between homophones and realise how spelling is integral to meaning. After they have finished the activity, hold a plenary session and ask them to share the sentences they wrote and compare how similar they are.

● **Photocopiable page 112 'Which option?'**
In this activity the children choose between pairs of sentences to find which one uses a confusable word correctly. They write the words in their spelling journal with their own definitions to help them to differentiate between the words. Before beginning the activity, ask the children to brainstorm some homophones that they already know. Point out that the sound of the word out

of context gives no clues to its meaning and so no clues to its spelling. Reinforce that understanding meaning is crucial to the correct use and, therefore, correct spelling.

● **Photocopiable page 113 'Know the meanings'**
In this activity the children write their own definition of commonly confused words, and they then write the dictionary definition and a sentence that uses the word correctly. As a follow-up activity to help them to consolidate their knowledge, ask them to identify the words they find tricky and encourage them to write a memory-jogger or mnemonic to help them remember. Suggest that they record these words and memory-joggers in their personal spelling journals.

Further ideas

● **Confusable cards:** Create word cards of the most easily confused words and place them face down. Work with a small group of children and invite the children, in turn, to pick a card. If they can use the word correctly in a sentence, the card can be removed. If used incorrectly it is replaced face down.

● **Circle time:** With a small group of children, draw up a list of four or five simple homophones (for example, *to*, *too* and *two*; *there*, *they're* and *their* and so on). Ask one child to use the first word in a sentence – for example, *I am going to school.* The next child should extend the sentence by adding *too* and the third child then adds a phrase or clause that includes *two*. Continue round the circle using the other homophones from the list.

What's on the CD-ROM

On the CD-ROM you will find:
● Printable versions of all three photocopiable pages.
● Answers to 'Which option?'.
● Interactive version of 'Which option?'.

Confusables

What's my definition?

■ Write a sentence for each of these words to show their meaning. Use a dictionary to help you.

accept _____

_____

except _____

_____

angel _____

_____

angle _____

_____

allusion _____

_____

illusion _____

_____

principle _____

_____

principal _____

_____

course _____

_____

coarse _____

Illustrations © 2009, Rupert Van Wyk/Beehive Illustration.

Name:

Confusables

Which option?

■ Read these pairs of sentences. Put a tick next to the correct use of the underlined word and then check your answer with a dictionary. The first is done as an example to help you.

1. Take care you don't **brake** the glass! ✗
   Take care you don't **break** the glass! ✔

2. The cross-country **course** was very challenging. ☐
   The cross-country **coarse** was very challenging. ☐

3. Danny ate the **whole** meal far too quickly and felt quite sick. ☐
   Danny ate the **hole** meal far too quickly and felt quite sick. ☐

4. She wrote a **draught** for her story before typing it on a computer. ☐
   She wrote a **draft** for her story before typing it on a computer. ☐

5. **Whose** shoes have been left in the cloakroom? ☐
   Who's shoes have been left in the cloakroom? ☐

6. The school **principal** made a speech to all the parents. ☐
   The school **principle** made a speech to all the parents. ☐

7. The building was **raised** to the ground. ☐
   The building was **razed** to the ground. ☐

8. You must **ensure** your work is finished by the end of today. ☐
   You must **insure** your work is finished by the end of today. ☐

9. Our **plane** will be taking off at 5.30 on Tuesday evening. ☐
   Our **plain** will be taking off at 5.30 on Tuesday evening. ☐

10. That was a lovely **complement** to make. Thank you. ☐
    That was a lovely **compliment** to make. Thank you. ☐

■ Copy each of the confusable words into your spelling journal and write your own definition for each one.

PHOTOCOPIABLE   ■SCHOLASTIC
www.scholastic.co.uk

Confusables

Know the meanings

■ Discuss the definition of the word with your partner and write it down in the grid before looking it up in a dictionary. Write the dictionary definition and then use the words in sentences on a piece of paper.

	My definition	Dictionary definition
descent		
decent		
dissent		
vain		
vein		
vane		
stationary		
stationery		
ascent		
accent		
loose		
lose		
site		
sight		

Editing, prefixes and suffixes

Objectives

To practise editing a passage of writing. To revise the conventions for adding prefixes 'un-', 'im-', 'mis-', 'dis-', and suffixes '-ness', '-ity' and '-y' to root words.

Background knowledge

Children often rely heavily on a spellchecker when using a computer to write. When they realise that the checker only picks up errors in spelling patterns and not errors in meaning and usage they become aware of the need to edit their work themselves. Knowledge of the conventions for adding prefixes and suffixes is fundamental to good spelling and in the activities in this section the children are given plenty of opportunities to practise their skills.

Activities

● **Photocopiable page 115 'Editing'**
In this activity the children reinforce their knowledge of the meaning and spelling of words by editing a passage with 22 errors and rewriting them correctly. Before giving copies of the page to the children, read the passage aloud to them and ask them if they understand it. Explain that although it sounds as if it is written correctly, it contains a number of errors that can only be found by reading it rather than listening to it.

● **Photocopiable page 116 'Revising prefixes'**
As the children change a passage from positive to negative by adding negative prefixes, they reinforce their knowledge of the spelling patterns when adding 'un-', 'im-', 'mis-' and 'dis-'. They extend their vocabulary further by finding synonyms for the words with negative prefixes. After completing the activity, hold a plenary session to compare the children's choices of alternative words. Ask some of the children to read the passage aloud while substituting the words with negative prefixes with their alternative words. For example: *The activities were dull and mostly dangerous*.

● **Photocopiable page 117 'Revisiting suffixes'**
In this activity the children add suffixes to change adjectives to nouns using '-ness', '-ity' and '-y'. Explain to the children that they need to think about how the spelling of the adjective will change when adding the correct suffix. Support less confident children by using *brief* as an example and asking: *Should we add the suffix '-ness' or '-ity', making 'briefness' or 'brevity'?* Encourage them to think about whether the root word needs to change, or just the final letter when words end in '-y'. Allow children who need support to use a dictionary to help them when they cannot decide between the suffixes '-ness' or '-ity'.

Further ideas

● **Prefix and suffix cards:** Make prefix and suffix cards to add to root word cards. Play games where the children need to add prefixes, suffixes or both to make new words.
● **Spellcheck:** Ask the children to type the passage from photocopiable page 115 on a computer and run the spellchecker to see which errors the checker picks up and which it misses. Ask them why the checker misses those errors.

What's on the CD-ROM

On the CD-ROM you will find:
● Printable versions of all three photocopiable pages.
● Answers to all three photocopiable pages.
● Interactive versions of 'Editing' and 'Revising prefixes'.

Editing, prefixes and suffixes

Editing

■ Read this passage carefully. There are 22 mistakes (spelling or incorrect use of words). Cross them out and write them correctly at the bottom of the page.

William Shakespeare was a righter of great reknown. He was both a playwrite and poet. He was born in 1564 in a plaice called Stratford-upon-Avon. Later he moved to London to work in the theater. The most famouse theatre was the Globe. It was bilt in a circle with an open roof. Audiences were'nt as well-behaved as they are today. They offen shouted and jeered at the players or through food at the stage. In Elizabethan times, women were not aloud to be acters so boys had to play the femail rolls. Many other aspects of life have changed sins Shakespeare lived. The way people spoke and spellt was diffrent fore hundred years ago so sometimes Shakespeare's language can be trickey to understand. However, because he rote about people and how they behave, his plays are still as poppular today as they where when they were first written.

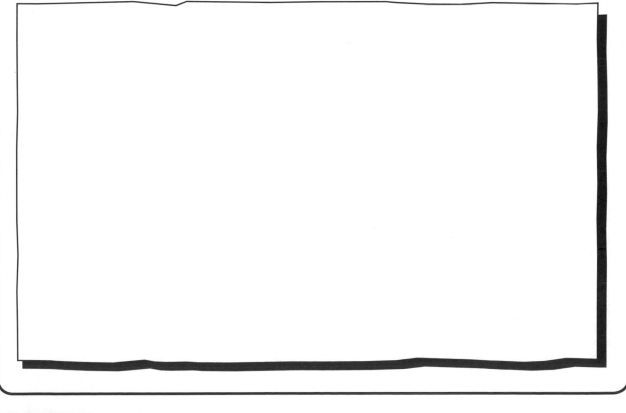

Name:

Revising prefixes

■ Use prefixes to change this recount of a school trip from positive to negative (for example, *polite* would become *impolite*). Write the new words in the spaces provided, and cross out the wrong one.

This year's school trip to the seaside was really _____ successful.

The children were _____ polite at all times. They _____

behaved themselves for most of the journey. This made it _____

pleasant for everyone. We arrived at an _____ timely hour and went

_____ happily to bed. The teachers _____ liked the

accommodation and thought the food was _____ edible. The activities

were _____ exciting and mostly _____ safe. Most of the

children are _____ likely to want to visit it again.

■ Fill in the table below with six of the negative words you have made, plus an alternative (such as *dull* or *boring* instead of *unexciting*).

Negative word	Alternative word

PHOTOCOPIABLE

SCHOLASTIC
www.scholastic.co.uk

Editing, prefixes and suffixes

Revisiting suffixes

■ Add a suffix to change these adjectives to nouns (for example, *happy* becomes *happiness*).

Adjective	Noun
lazy	
clear	
bright	
choppy	
brief	
soft	
scarce	
able	
wary	
flexible	
damp	
difficult	
pretty	
tricky	

■ Think of a rule to help you spell nouns made from adjectives.

_____

_____

Illustrations © 2009, Rupert Van Wyk/Beehive Illustration.

■ SCHOLASTIC   **PHOTOCOPIABLE**
www.scholastic.co.uk

Memory-joggers

Objective

Objective

To use mnemonics as an aid to remember how to spell words.

Background knowledge

Mnemonics can be used in many different ways to jog your memory. Acrostic mnemonics (a phrase or sentence made from the initial letters of the word), work well if they are unusual or humorous. Encourage the children to illustrate the acrostic in their mind's eye and to draw the picture next to their invented acrostic. Other ideas can be a sentence using the tricky part of the word, rhymes and pictures. When children make up their own mnemonics they are more likely to remember them.

Activities

● **Photocopiable page 119 'What are they?'**
In this activity the children are asked to make up memory-jogging acrostics to help them spell words with unstressed vowels. Before beginning the activity, remind the children of the work they did in Chapter 4 on mnemonics. Ask them if they remember any of the mnemonics they wrote (or ask them to look back at the work they did). Which mnemonics were the most memorable – those that reflected the meaning of the word (for example, *Rhythm Has Your Two Hips Moving*) or the funny ones, such as *Big Elephants Can Always Understand Small Elephants*?

● **Photocopiable page 120 'Mnemonics'**
The children make up mnemonics for some commonly misspelled words and add tricky words of their own from their spelling logs. When they have completed the activity, hold a plenary session and ask them to read the mnemonics from the photocopiable sheet. Discuss how similar or different they are and ask them to suggest which ones will be the most helpful to them. Compare which personal tricky words they chose and compile a list of any tricky words they had in common.

● **Photocopiable page 121 'Stress the consonants'**
As the children look for unstressed consonants in words, they write or draw their own way of remembering it. Before handing out copies of the photocopiable sheet, read the list of words to the children and ask them if they can hear all the letters in the spoken words or if they think there are any unstressed letters. Read the list again, this time over-pronouncing the unstressed letter.

Further ideas

● **Mnemonic memory:** Write a daily mnemonic on the board and chant it together during the day. Erase it at the end of the day and ask the children to chant it from memory.
● **Display:** Choose some of the more amusing or memorable memory-joggers and make a decorated wall display.

What's on the CD-ROM

On the CD-ROM you will find:
● Printable versions of all three photocopiable pages.

Memory-joggers

What are they?

■ Write your own memory-jogger acrostics for these words with unstressed vowels (for example, *Ocean: Ordinary Children Eat Apples Nicely*).

patient

p _____

a _____

t _____

i _____

e _____

n _____

t _____

history

h _____

i _____

s _____

t _____

o _____

r _____

y _____

enough

e _____

n _____

o _____

u _____

g _____

h _____

benefit

b _____

e _____

n _____

e _____

f _____

i _____

t _____

queue

q _____

u _____

e _____

u _____

e _____

January

J _____

a _____

n _____

u _____

a _____

r _____

y _____

Illustrations © 2009, Rupert Van Wyk/Beehive Illustration.

Name:

Memory-joggers

Mnemonics

■ Invent your own mnemonics for these tricky words.

■ Then look at your spelling log and add mnemonics for the words you always find tricky. For example: *accommodation – a room with two cots and two mattresses* (two **c**s and two **m**s).

affect _____

_____

effect _____

_____

bargain _____

_____

business _____

_____

hear _____

_____

here _____

_____

necessary _____

_____

separate _____

_____

PHOTOCOPIABLE   **■SCHOLASTIC**
www.scholastic.co.uk

Memory-joggers

Stress the consonants

■ These words all have consonants that are not stressed when they are spoken.

■ Circle the unstressed consonant, then think of a memory-jogger to help you remember it. This can be an acrostic, a rhyme – or even a picture. Write or draw your memory-jogger in the box.

dustbin	
raspberry	
cupboard	
postpone	
government	
February	
handbag	
Wednesday	

Assessment

Assessment grid

The following grid shows the main objectives and activities covered in this chapter. You can use the grid to locate activities that cover a particular focus that you are keen to monitor.

Objective	Page	Activity title
To secure the spelling and meaning of easily confused words.	**111** **112** **113**	What's my definition? Which option? Know the meanings
To practise editing a passage of writing. To revise the conventions for adding prefixes 'un-', 'im-', 'mis-', 'dis-', and suffixes '-ness', '-ity' and '-y' to root words.	**115** **116** **117**	Editing Revising prefixes Revisiting suffixes
To use mnemonics as an aid to remember how to spell words.	**119** **120** **121**	What are they? Mnemonics Stress the consonants

Observation and record keeping

This assessment activity involves the children in editing a school newsletter which contains 28 mistakes. The errors are all in words that the children have been focusing on throughout all seven chapters, including prefixes and suffixes, commonly misspelled words and homophones, capital letters and apostrophe use. It provides an opportunity to observe whether children need to revise certain rules and strategies further.

While the children are completing the photocopiable sheets in this chapter, encourage them to keep a spelling journal, for example, recording how well they did and any difficulties they encountered. Encourage them to write down any words that were tricky for them and any mistakes they made. A note of appropriate rules, patterns and mnemonics will also be helpful to them.

For example:

Tricky words	I wrote	Rule	Correct spelling
laziness	lazyness	change 'y' to 'i' when adding a suffix	laziness

Assessment activity

● **What you need**
Photocopiable page 123 'Spot the mistakes', writing materials.
● **What to do**
Read the newsletter aloud before giving it to the children. Explain that there are 28 errors in the letter. Challenge the children to find the errors, cross them out in the passage and then neatly write the correction above the mistake.

Differentiation

● Explain to less confident learners what errors to look out for. For example, tell them to check for mistakes in words with unstressed vowels, homophones, capitalisation, negative prefixes, suffixes, words with double consonants and plurals. Make sure that they understand the terminology you are using.
● Give groups of more confident learners a time limit to complete the assessment task.

Further learning

● **Quiz:** Using the pairs of homophones and confusable words, ask the children to choose three pairs of words each and create a class quiz. Each child writes a clue about one word's spelling and meaning for each of their three pairs of words. Pool their clues and hold a quiz. Provide the children with whiteboards and pens. Arrange them into small mixed-ability groups to play against each other in a timed competition. Read some mnemonics aloud to the children without letting them see the written word. The group who all write the correct word on their boards in the shortest time wins. This encourages the children to collaborate and help each other.

Assessment

Spot the mistakes

■ There are 28 mistakes in this school newsletter. Draw a line through each mistake and write the correction above the error.

Summer Fair Announcement

Dear parent's

The school summer fare will be held on Saturday the 15th of August. The school principle will make a short speech to intraduce our spccial gest, the reknowned children's author, May Kerovtales, who will open the fair at approxematly two o'clock. Counciler Smith and the Mayor will also be in attendence.

Among the many attracions will be a bouncy castle, a fire engine, a fire-eater and magicion. (The fire engine might be helpfull to the fire-eater!) As usuall we will be having book and cake stalls and would welcome you're contributians.

In the mislikely event of unclement weather, many of the entertainments will be held in the mane hall. However, I surgest you bring an umbrela to be on the safe side.

The entrie fee is £2 for adults but it is free for childrcn. Wc will be holding some games and races for childs and parents so insure you bring your trainers on the day.

We are all looking forewords to a fun-picked afternoon and hope all parents and children will atend.

Yours sinceerly

Mrs Miller

School secritry

General activities

How to use the general activities

These activities can be used in a flexible way to support your spelling programme. It includes a range of games, ten-minute group and whole-class activities and circle times, all linked to the work in this book. You may choose to use the games and activities as warm-ups, plenary sessions or as part of your main lesson. The five-minute ideas on page 127 are intended to be used as mental warm-ups or plenary sessions. Words can be selected to meet current needs, such as high frequency words, topic words, or words with particular letter strings, affixes or spelling rules. They can be played with the whole class or with a group. They encourage quick response and reinforce the skill of spelling from memory or 'in your mind's eye'. Individual whiteboards could be used to try spellings in most of the games if appropriate.

What's the consonant?

Linked activities:
Chapter 1: page 16
Chapter 3: pages 44, 48
Chapter 4: page 60

What to do

- A teacher or a child chooses a word but doesn't tell the class or group what it is. (A child may want to write the word to check spelling and keep it hidden.)
- The teacher or child writes only the vowels on the whiteboard with dashes to indicate the missing consonants. The rest of the group have to work out what the word is by guessing the missing consonants. If a word uses the same consonant more than once, each correctly guessed consonant only counts as one, for example, for the word *attentive* when 't' is suggested it should be added once *at_ e _ _ i _ e*.
- The children can take turns individually or work in groups collaboratively.
- Encourage them to think of possible letter sequences, drawing on knowledge of digraphs, adjacent consonants and common letter strings.
- Another variation can be to focus on missing vowels rather than missing consonants.

Spell a word

Linked activities:
Any of the chapters in the book.

What to do

- Provide the children with a list of words, letter tiles (with values per letter) and boards with grids on them (include special squares, such as five bonus points).
- Tell them to spell out each word using the letter tiles and work out their numerical values, for example, *extreme* might have a value of 16, but a longer word, *delicious* only has a value of 12.
- Ask the children to work in small groups. Tell each group to arrange the words from the list on the board in the fashion of a crossword. Using the special squares, each group tries to get the highest total score for the word list.

What's my word?

Linked activities:
Chapter 1: page 12
Chapter 2: pages 32, 36
Chapter 3: pages 48, 52
Chapter 4: pages 65, 70
Chapter 5: page 78
Chapter 6: page 102

What to do

● Select a list of words you want the children to revise. Display the word list.

● Ask the children to choose one word from the list. Tell them to investigate their chosen word by taking it apart and putting it back together again.

● Invite them to write the word on their whiteboards. Ask them to say the word out loud and count the syllables. Tell them to underline the syllables on their whiteboards.

● Next, count the phonemes and write the number next to the word.

● Then tell them to look for prefixes, suffixes and root words. Encourage them to look for spelling rules and mnemonics that apply to their chosen word and any other features, for example, double consonants, digraphs, silent letters, word origins and meaning.

● When they have had sufficient time to investigate the word thoroughly, tell them to write their findings in no more than two sentences on a strip of paper and erase their whiteboards. The sentences are to act as a clue to the word.

● Ask the children to take turns to come to the front and read out their clues. The rest of the children try to work out what the word is and write it down and hold up their whiteboards.

Syllable race

Linked activities:
Chapter 1: pages 12, 16
Chapter 3: page 52
Chapter 4: page 60
Chapter 5: pages 78, 82, 86
Chapter 6: pages 94, 98
Chapter 7: page 114

What to do

● Arrange the children into small mixed-ability teams, preferably with each around a table. Appoint a secretary for each team.

● Write a syllable on the board. Each member of each team writes as many words as possible containing the syllable on their own whiteboard within a limited time.

● When the time is up, the teams should count up the total number of words that the whole group has written and spelled correctly. Any duplicate words only count as one.

● Each team secretary should then write the team list on a whiteboard and hold it up for all the other teams to see.

● Other teams can challenge words and if they are incorrect they should be wiped off the list.

● The team that has written the most correct words within the time wins.

● Extend the game by writing a letter string on the board rather than syllables, for example, the teams write as many words containing the letters 'ious' as they can within the time limit.

Play or pass

Linked activities:
Any of the chapters in the book.

What to do

● Select a number of words you want the children to revise or that they frequently spell wrongly. You need an appropriate number of words so that there are at least two words for each child in the group.

● Arrange the children in a circle.

● Ask the first child (child 1) in the circle to spell a particular word. The child can choose to play or pass. If child 1 chooses to play, they must spell the word correctly to get a point. If child 1 chooses to pass, they pass the word to the child next to them (child 2). Child 2 must then attempt to spell the word. The word can no longer be passed. If child 2 spells it correctly, they win the point. If child 2 spells it incorrectly, the point is awarded to child 1.

● Now ask child 2 to spell a new word. Child 2 can now choose to play or pass. If child 2 chooses to pass, child 3 must attempt the word. If child 2 chooses to play and spells the word correctly, child 2 wins the point.

● Then you ask child 3 to spell a different word. If child 3 chooses to pass, child 4 must attempt the word. If child 4 spells it correctly, they win the point. If child 4 gets it wrong, the point is awarded to child 3. Then you ask child 4 to spell a new word.

● Continue around the group until all the words you have chosen have been spelled.

Spelling relay

Linked activities:
Any of the chapters in the book.

What to do

● Prepare three lists of words with different levels of challenge, give them headings, A, B or C. Write them on a board or pin them to a wall. Allocate points for each word list according to the challenge, for example, 'A' words are worth 2 points, 'B' words are worth 4 points and 'C' words are worth 10 points.

● Arrange the children into two mixed teams in two lines facing the board. Allow them a few minutes to become familiar with the words on the board.

● The first child from each team (the speller) stands with her back to the board so that she cannot see the word lists. The next child from each team asks this child to choose a list, A, B or C and asks her to spell one word from it. If it is spelled correctly, the team wins the points, the word is crossed out and the speller joins the team at the back of the line. If the child gets it wrong, there is no score.

● The next child now at the front becomes the speller and stands at the front facing the team. Continue until all the words have been crossed out.

● The team with the highest score is the winner.

● To vary this game, give each team one list only that consists of the same words of mixed difficulty. The teams must spell the words on the list and cross out the words when they are spelled correctly. The winning team is the first team to cross out all the words on their list.

Five-minute ideas

Spelling A B C

● Choose a word and write it in alphabetical order on the board, for example, 'underneath' becomes 'adeehnnrtu'. Ask the children to make as many words as they can, like this, in a limited time. Give them points for the most words and bonus points if anyone finds the whole original word.

Newspaper spelling

● Arrange the children into groups of three. Provide them with sheets of newspaper. Call out a word and the children have to tear out letters and put them together to make the word. The group that succeeds and spells it correctly first wins.

● Back to back spelling

● Arrange the children so that they are standing in a circle. Choose someone and tell him to use a finger to write a word on their neighbour's back. The neighbour must then say the word aloud. If he gets it wrong he drops out and the first one has another turn. If he gets it right he then writes on the next child's back and so on.

Missing letter race

● Arrange the children in groups, give each child a number and provide each group with a set of magnetic letters. Write a word on a magnetic board with one letter missing. The groups find the missing magnetic letter and child 1 from each group tries to be the first to put it into place. Write another word on the board and miss out two letters. Children 2 and 3 from each group try to be the first to put them into place. Continue until you finish with a word that has only one letter written on the board. To avoid children bumping into each other, place a marker before the board and the first child to reach it is allowed to put the letter on the board.

Find my family

● Prepare a set of root words, prefix and suffix cards. Divide the root cards between four or five children. Give the remaining children a suffix card or a prefix card. Ask one of the root card holders to stand at the front and the rest of the children read their cards. If they can make a word in the same family they come and join the root. Each one should say and spell their word.

Spelling consequences

● Arrange the children into groups of five or six. Give each of the groups a strip of paper. Choose one child in each group to begin. Ask her to think of a word with the same number of letters as group members, without telling the group what it is, and write the first letter on the strip of paper. The strip is then passed from child to child with each child adding a letter that could follow the letter or letters already written. When they have all had a turn, ask the first child to say the word they had thought of and read the word on the completed strip.

● As a variation, give the children a strip of paper with a three letter word written on it and fold over the first letter. The strip is passed around the group and each group member looks at the two showing letters and adds a letter to the word. When everyone has had a turn, they read their result. Is it a real word or a nonsense word?

Also available in this series:

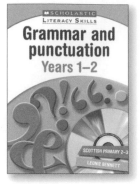

ISBN 978-1407-10045-6

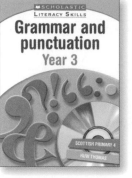

ISBN 978-1407-10046-3

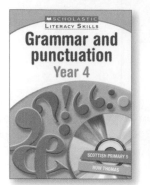

ISBN 978-1407-10047-0

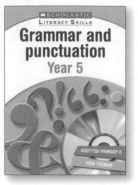

ISBN 978-1407-10048-7

ISBN 978-1407-10049-4

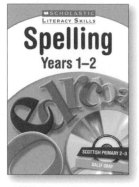

ISBN 978-1407-10055-5

ISBN 978-1407-10056-2

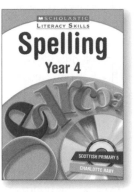

ISBN 978-1407-10057-9

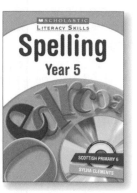

ISBN 978-1407-10058-6

ISBN 978-1407-10059-3

ISBN 978-1407-10050-0

ISBN 978-1407-10051-7

ISBN 978-1407-10052-4

ISBN 978-1407-10053-1

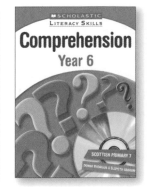

ISBN 978-1407-10054-8

ISBN 978-1407-10223-8

ISBN 978-1407-10224-5

ISBN 978-1407-10225-2

ISBN 978-1407-10226-9

ISBN 978-1407-10227-6

To find out more, call: 0845 603 9091
or visit our website www.scholastic.co.uk